Preliminary Assessment of Channel Stability and Bed-Material Transport in the Coquille River Basin, Southwestern Oregon

By Krista L. Jones, Jim E. O'Connor, Mackenzie K. Keith, Joseph F. Mangano, and J. Rose Wallick

Prepared in cooperation with the U.S. Army Corps of Engineers and the Oregon Department of State Lands

Open-File Report 2012–1064

U.S. Department of the Interior
U.S. Geological Survey

U.S. Department of the Interior
KEN SALAZAR, Secretary

U.S. Geological Survey
Marcia K. McNutt, Director

U.S. Geological Survey, Reston, Virginia 2012

For more information on the USGS—the Federal source for science about the Earth, its natural and living resources, natural hazards, and the environment, visit http://www.usgs.gov or call 1–888–ASK–USGS.

For an overview of USGS information products, including maps, imagery, and publications, visit http://www.usgs.gov/pubprod

To order this and other USGS information products, visit http://store.usgs.govFor more information on the USGS—the Federal source for science about the Earth,
its natural and living resources, natural hazards, and the environment:
World Wide Web: http://www.usgs.gov
Telephone: 1-888-ASK-USGS

Suggested citation:
Jones, K.L., O'Connor, J.E., Keith, M.K., Mangano, J.F., and Wallick, J.R., 2012, Preliminary assessment of channel stability and bed-material transport in the Coquille River basin, southwestern Oregon: U.S. Geological Survey Open-File Report 2012–1064, 84 p.

Any use of trade, product, or firm names is for descriptive purposes only and does not imply endorsement by the U.S. Government.

Contents

Figures

Tables

Conversion Factors

Multiply	By	To obtain
Length		
centimeter (cm)	0.3937	inch (in.)
millimeter (mm)	0.03937	inch (in.)
meter (m)	3.281	foot (ft)
kilometer (km)	0.6214	mile (mi)
Area		
square meter (m^2)	10.76	square foot (ft^2)
square kilometer (km^2)	0.3861	square mile (mi^2)
Volume		
cubic meter (m^3)	0.0008107	acre-foot (acre-ft)
cubic meter (m^3)	35.31	cubic foot (ft^3)
cubic meter (m^3)	1.308	cubic yard (yd^3)
Flow rate		
cubic meter per second (m^3/s)	35.31	cubic foot per second (ft^3/s)
cubic meter per year (m^3/yr)	1.308	cubic yard per year (yd^3/yr)
meter per second (m/s)	3.281	foot per second (ft/s)
Mass		
kilogram (kg)	2.205	pound avoirdupois (lb)

Datums

Vertical coordinate information is referenced to the North American Vertical Datum of 1988 (NAVD 88).

Horizontal coordinate information is referenced to the North American Datum of 1983 (NAD 83).

Elevation, as used in this report, refers to distance above the vertical datum.

Preliminary Assessment of Channel Stability and Bed-Material Transport in the Coquille River Basin, Southwestern Oregon

By Krista L. Jones, Jim E. O'Connor, Mackenzie K. Keith, Joseph F. Mangano, and J. Rose Wallick

Significant Findings

This report summarizes a preliminary study of bed-material transport, vertical and lateral channel changes, and existing datasets for the Coquille River basin, which encompasses 2,745 km² (square kilometers) of the southwestern Oregon coast. This study, conducted to inform permitting decisions regarding instream gravel mining, revealed that:

- The 115.4-km-long study area on the South Fork and mainstem Coquille River can be divided into four reaches on the basis of topography and hydrology. In the fluvial (nontidal, or dominated by riverine processes) reaches on the South Fork Coquille River, the channel consists of bedrock and alluvium in the Powers Reach and mostly alluvium in the Broadbent Reach. In both fluvial reaches, the channel alternates between confined and unconfined segments and contains gravel bars. In the tidally affected Myrtle Point and Bandon Reaches, the channel consists of alluvial deposits and contains sparse gravel and sand bars as well as expansive mud flats and tidal marshes near the Coquille River mouth.

- The 15.4- and 14.6-km-long study areas on the Middle and North Forks of the Coquille River, respectively, were treated as distinct reaches. The channel beds consist of mixed bedrock and alluvium in the Bridge Reach on the Middle Fork Coquille River and alluvium in the Gravelford Reach on the North Fork Coquille River. Both of these reaches contain fewer bars than the Powers and Broadbent Reaches on the South Fork Coquille River and are predominately fluvial.

- Channel condition, bed-material transport, and the distribution and area of bars have likely been influenced by logging and splash damming, dredging and wood removal for navigation, historical and ongoing instream gravel mining, gold mining, fires, and mass movements. These anthropogenic and natural disturbances likely have varying effects on channel condition and sediment flux throughout the study area and over time.

- Available data include at least eight sets of aerial and orthophotographs that were taken of the study area from 1939 to 2011 that are available for assessing long-term changes in channel condition, bar area, and vegetation establishment patterns. Additionally, a high-resolution Light Detection And Ranging (LiDAR) survey conducted in 2008 for nearly the entire study area would be useful in future quantitative analyses of channel morphology and bed-material transport.

- Previous studies found (1) substantial bank erosion in the Broadbent Reach, resulting in banks with near vertical profiles and heights exceeding 7.6 m, (2) erosion of over 40,000 square meters of riparian land from 1939 to 1992, (3) incision along the South Fork Coquille River, and (4) potential for lateral channel migration at several locations along the mainstem and South Fork Coquille River.

- A review of deposited and mined bed-material estimates derived largely from repeat surveys at instream mining sites on the South

Fork Coquille River indicates that bed material transported by the river tends to rebuild mined bar surfaces in most years. Reported annual deposition volumes for 1996–2009 indicate average transport of over 34,700 cubic meters per year (m^3/yr) of bed material into the South Fork Coquille River study area.

- The spatial variation in the number and area of gravel bars is controlled by factors such as valley confinement, channel slope, basin geology, and tidal extent. The Powers and Broadbent Reaches of the South Fork Coquille River have the greatest abundance of gravel bars, likely owing to a substantial area of the South Fork Coquille River basin draining the gravel-producing Klamath Mountains geologic province.

- From 1939 to 2009, the fluvial reaches all had a net loss in bar area, ranging from 24 percent in the Powers Reach to 56 percent in the Bridge Reach. In the Powers and Broadbent Reaches, the declines in active bar area were associated primarily with vegetation establishment on bar surfaces and lateral bar erosion. The reductions in active bar area were attributed to vegetation establishment in the Bridge and Gravelford Reaches as well as some lateral bar erosion in the Bridge Reach.

- In contrast, the tidal Myrtle Point and Bandon Reaches had a net increase in bar area (28 and 29 percent, respectively) from 1939 to 2009. In the Myrtle Point Reach, these increases in bar area were primarily attributed to lateral channel migration that led to the deposition of bed material at newly formed bars. In the Bandon Reach, bar area increased primarily in the lower 5.4 km of the reach owing possibly to factors such as tide differences between the photographs and sediment deposition.

- Analyses of multiple channel cross sections along the South Fork Coquille River as well as historical stage-discharge data collected by the U.S. Geological Survey (USGS) at Powers, Oregon, indicate that the bed of the South Fork Coquille River has locally lowered, as

much as 1.9 m from 1994 to 2008 for one site in the Broadbent Reach. Stage-discharge data indicate persistent incision at the Powers site since 1939 (with a net incision of about 0.3 m) that has been interrupted by episodic aggradation apparently corresponding with large floods.

- For the Bridge and Gravelford Reaches on the Middle and North Forks of the Coquille River, channel cross sections indicate a mix of aggradation and incision as well as bank erosion and deposition from 1992 to 2010 and 2000 to 2009, respectively.

- Cross sections in the tidal reaches indicate local incision of 0.4 m in at one site in the Myrtle Point Reach from 2004 to 2008 and 0.5 m at one site in in the Bandon Reach from 2000 to 2010.

- On the South Fork Coquille River, the median diameter of surface particles varied from 78.0 mm (millimeters) at China Flat Bar slightly upstream of the study area to 48.8 mm at Seals Bar in the Broadbent Reach. The armoring ratio (or ratio of the median grain sizes of the surface and subsurface layers) for Seals Bar was 3.5, indicating that the river's transport capacity likely exceeds sediment supply at this site.

- Most fluvial reaches in the Coquille River study area are likely supply-limited, meaning that the river's transport capacity exceeds the supply of bed-material, as indicated by the intermittent bedrock outcrops in the Powers and Bridge Reaches and the paucity of bars in the Bridge and Gravelford Reaches.

- The Broadbent Reach of the South Fork Coquille River may be presently and probably was historically transport-limited, meaning that bed-material transport is primarily a function of local transport capacity. However, the locally coarse bed texture, high armoring ratio measured at Seals Bar, and recent channel incision indicate that sediment supply has likely diminished relative to transport capacity in recent decades.

- Because of exceedingly low gradients, the tidal Myrtle Point and Bandon Reaches are transport limited. Bed material in these reaches is primarily sand and finer grain-size material, much of which is probably transported as suspended load from upstream reaches. The tidal reaches will be most susceptible to watershed conditions affecting the supply and transport of fine sediment.

- Compared to the nearby Chetco and Rogue Rivers and Hunter Creek on the southwestern Oregon coast, the Coquille River likely has lower overall transport of gravel bed material. While the conclusion of lower bed-material transport in the Coquille River is tentative in the absence of actual transport measurements or transport capacity calculations, empirical evidence including the much lower area and frequency of bars for most of the Coquille River study area and the head of tide reaching to RKM (river kilometer) 63.2 on the South Fork Coquille River supports this conclusion.

- More detailed investigations of bed-material transport rates and channel morphology would support assessments of lateral and vertical channel condition and longitudinal trends in bed material. Such assessments would be most practical for the Powers and Broadbent Reaches and relevant to several ongoing management and ecological issues pertaining to sand and gravel transport. The tidal Bandon and Myrtle Point Reaches may also be logical subjects for in-depth analyses of fine sediment deposition and transport (and associated channel and riparian conditions and processes) rather than coarse bed material.

Introduction

This report summarizes a reconnaissance-level study of channel condition and bed-material transport relevant to the permitting of instream gravel mining in the Coquille River basin (fig. 1). This assessment is based on a review of existing datasets (such as channel cross sections and instream gravel mining records), delineation of bar and channel features over time from aerial and orthophotographs, and field observations and bed-material measurements made in July 2010. Findings from these datasets and observations in the Coquille River basin were used to (1) identify key datasets and issues that are relevant to understanding channel condition, bed-material transport, and potential effects of instream gravel mining, and (2) assess the vertical and lateral stability of river segments and identify locations where channels may be incising, aggrading, prone to migration, or stable. This reconnaissance-level study constitutes a "Phase I" assessment similar to those completed in the Umpqua River (O'Connor and others, 2009), Hunter Creek (Jones and others, 2011), and Rogue River (Jones and others, 2012) basins, in cooperation with the U.S. Army Corps of Engineers (hereafter Corps of Engineers) and the Oregon Department of State Lands to inform the permitting of instream gravel mining in Oregon.

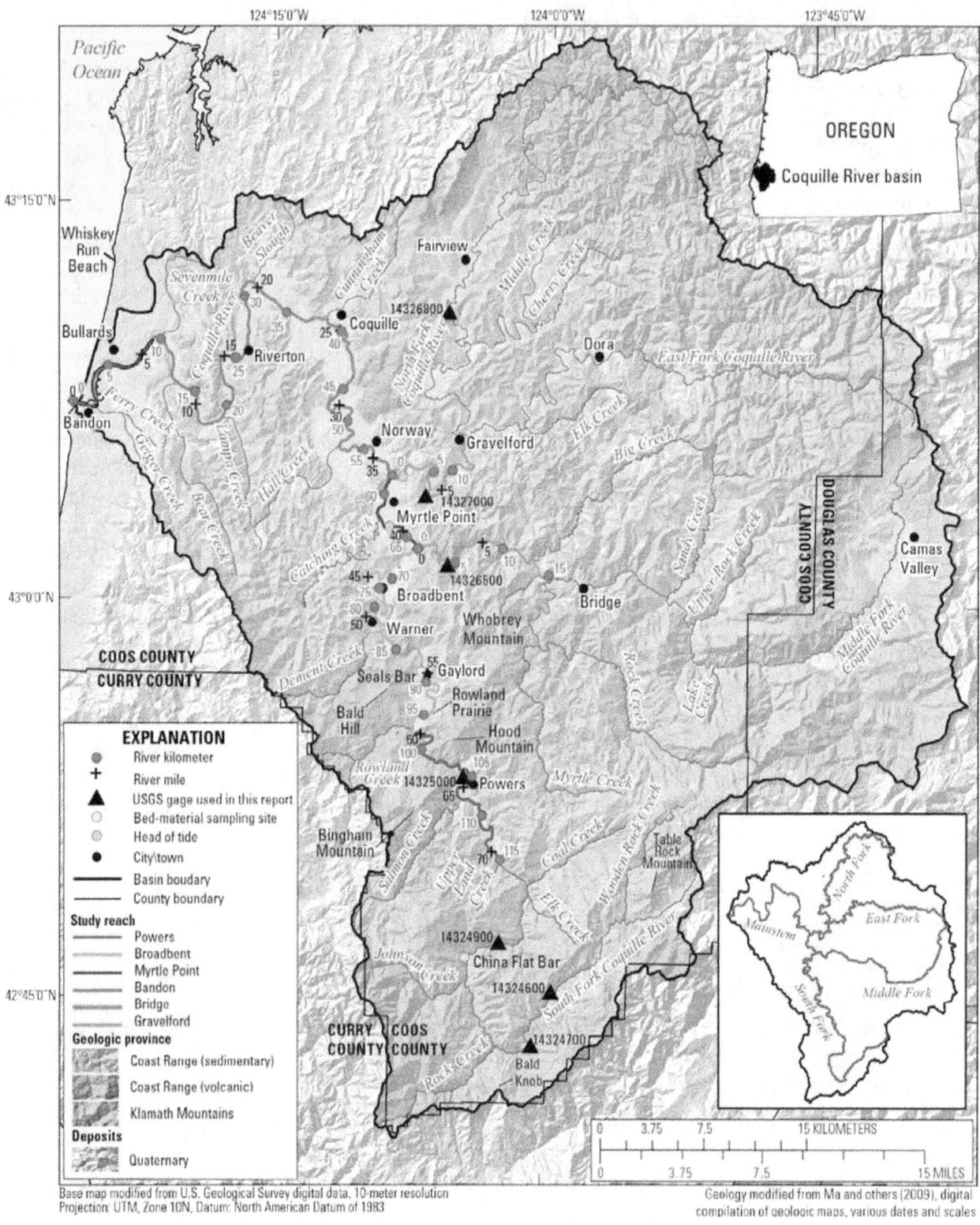

Figure 1. Map displaying the stream network, basin and county boundaries, geologic provinces, study reaches, linear reference systems, and streamflow gage used in this study of the Coquille River basin, southwestern Oregon.

Locations and Reporting Units

Locations along the Coquille River and its forks (the North, Middle, and South Forks of the Coquille River) within the study area are referenced to river kilometers (RKM). To develop this reference system, centerlines were digitized for the wetted channels of the Coquille River and its forks using orthoimagery taken in 2009 by the U.S. Department of Agriculture's (USDA) National Agriculture Imagery Program (NAIP). Points were distributed at 0.2-km intervals along these centerlines, starting at the downstream end of the jetties at the Coquille River mouth and continuing upstream along the South Fork Coquille River and then starting at the mouths of the Middle and North Forks of the Coquille River (fig. 1). Even after accounting for the conversion between river miles (RM) shown on current (1987, 1988, 1990, and 1991) USGS quadrangle maps and river kilometers developed by this study, these two reference systems differ slightly (fig. 1) owing to factors such as channel shifting and starting points of the linear reference systems.

Prominent landmarks and locations within the study area (from up- to downstream) include the confluences of the South and Middle Forks of the Coquille River (RKM 66.2), South and North Forks of the Coquille River (RKM 58.5), and North and East Forks of the Coquille River (North Fork Coquille River, RKM 14.8). The head of tide extends up the South Fork Coquille River to approximately RKM 63.2 and up the North Fork Coquille River to approximately RKM 0.9. Towns within the study area include Powers (South Fork Coquille River, RKM 106.3), Gaylord (South Fork Coquille River, RKM 89.4), Broadbent (South Fork Coquille River, RKM 75.2), Bridge (Middle Fork Coquille River, RKM 13.6), Gravelford (North Fork Coquille River, RKM 14.8), Myrtle Point (South Fork Coquille River, RKM 60.4), Coquille (mainstem, RKM 39.6), and Bandon (mainstem, RKM 1.4).

Names for the study reaches were assigned based on names of nearby towns or cities. Names for bed-material sampling sites were derived from USGS topographic maps or gravel-mining permits.

In this publication, we present all data collected and analyzed by this study as well as most data reported by other sources in metric, or SI, units. The conversions to English units are provided in the report front matter.

The Coquille River

The Coquille River system is an unregulated system that encompasses 2,745 km^2 of southwestern Oregon and flows into the Pacific Ocean near the town of Bandon (fig. 1). Over 1,963 kilometers of mapped channels make up the Coquille River network (StreamStats, *http://water.usgs.gov/osw/streamstats*). The Coquille River has four major forks, the South, Middle, East, and North Forks (fig. 1). Beginning in the Rogue River-Siskiyou National Forest, the South Fork Coquille River gains the Middle Fork Coquille River (drainage area 798 km^2) and shortly thereafter the North Fork Coquille River (749 km^2) (fig. 1). The East Fork Coquille River (347 km^2) joins the North Fork Coquille River near the town of Gravelford. Downstream of the confluence of the South and North Forks of the Coquille River, the mainstem Coquille River meanders westward to the coast. The Coquille River basin is located within Coos, Douglas, and Curry Counties in Oregon. The basin is flanked to the north by the Coos River basin, to the east by the South Umpqua River basin, to the south by the Rogue River basin, and to the southwest by the several smaller coastal basins, including Floras Creek and the Sixes and Elk Rivers.

Geographic, Geologic, and Geomorphic Setting

The South Fork Coquille River begins near Table Rock Mountain and flows southwestward for 26 km until reaching Bald Knob, where it turns northward for 22 km, gaining Rock (35 km^2), Johnson (42 km^2), Elk (13 km^2), Coal (40 km^2), and Upper Land Creeks (10 km^2; fig. 1). The study area on the South Fork Coquille River begins at RKM 115.4, slightly downstream of its confluence with Upper Land Creek. From here, the South Fork Coquille River continues generally northwestward for 49 km, gaining Salmon (58 km^2, RKM 107.4), Rowland (25 km^2, RKM 96.9), and Dement Creeks (38 km^2, RKM 82.4) before its confluence at RKM 66.2 with the westward flowing Middle Fork Coquille River (798 km^2; fig. 1). Downstream of the Middle Fork Coquille River, the South Fork Coquille River is joined by Catching Creek (81 km^2, RKM 61.8) and shortly thereafter by the southward flowing North Fork Coquille River (749 km^2) at RKM 58.5 (fig. 1). The mainstem Coquille River then winds westward for its last 58.5 km through the Coquille Valley, where the floodplain widens as it traverses coastal marine terrace deposits. Several small tributaries, including Hall Creek (37 km^2, RKM 52.5), Cunningham Creek (40 km^2, RKM 38.2), and Beaver Slough (38 km^2, RKM 31.5), join the Coquille River in this section. The lowermost 63.2 km of the South Fork and mainstem Coquille River and 0.9 km of the North Fork Coquille River are tidally influenced (Oregon Department of State Lands, 2007).

The Coquille River basin is primarily in the Oregon Coast Range, with the river flowing for its last 10 km through a sequence of coastal terraces that flank the coastline (fig. 1). The Klamath Mountains geologic province underlies 13 percent of the basin. The Coast Range geologic province covers approximately 76 percent of the basin, and includes the sedimentary (primarily Tertiary sedimentary rocks; 74 percent) and volcanic (2 percent) subdivisions. Mapped Quaternary sedimentary deposits and landslides make up 12 percent of the basin. The Klamath Mountains province primarily underlies the South Fork Coquille River and to a lesser extent the Middle Fork Coquille River. The sedimentary subdivision of the Coast Range dominates the drainages of the Middle and North Forks of the Coquille River, whereas Quaternary terraces and floodplains flank the channel in the Myrtle Point and Bandon Reaches. These diverse geologic environments reflect unique geologic histories and

conditions, resulting in distinct characteristics such as basin relief, drainage density, erosion processes, and water permeability that are relevant to sediment yield and transport.

Within the Coquille River basin, water surface gradient in the headwater sections for each of the main forks are variable and locally steep (fig. 2). Channel gradient, however, declines as the forks converge and then abruptly flattens in the tidally affected and lowermost 63.2 km of the river (fig. 2; fig. 3A–C). This far-inland gradient discontinuity indicates that the rate of gravel transported from the Coquille River to the Pacific Ocean has likely not kept pace with Holocene sea-level rise. In this respect, the Coquille River is similar to the many Coast Range drainages that have extensive tidal reaches (Komar, 1997), but contrasts with rivers of apparently high gravel supply such as the Chetco River (Wallick and others, 2010), Hunter Creek (Jones and others, 2011), and the Rogue River (Jones and others, 2012), which all have graded profiles to the coast and tidally affected sections less than 7 km long.

Hydrology

The USGS has measured streamflow at seven gages in the Coquille River basin for periods ranging from 13 to 91 years (table 1; *http://waterdata.usgs.gov/or/nwis/*). As of 2011, however, the only operating USGS streamflow-gaging station is on the South Fork Coquille River at Powers, Oregon (Powers gage, 14325000; fig. 1). Additionally, a search of the USGS National Water Information System (NWIS; *http://waterdata.usgs.gov/nwis*) database indicates that the USGS has not collected bedload or suspended load sediment samples in the Coquille River basin as of 2011.

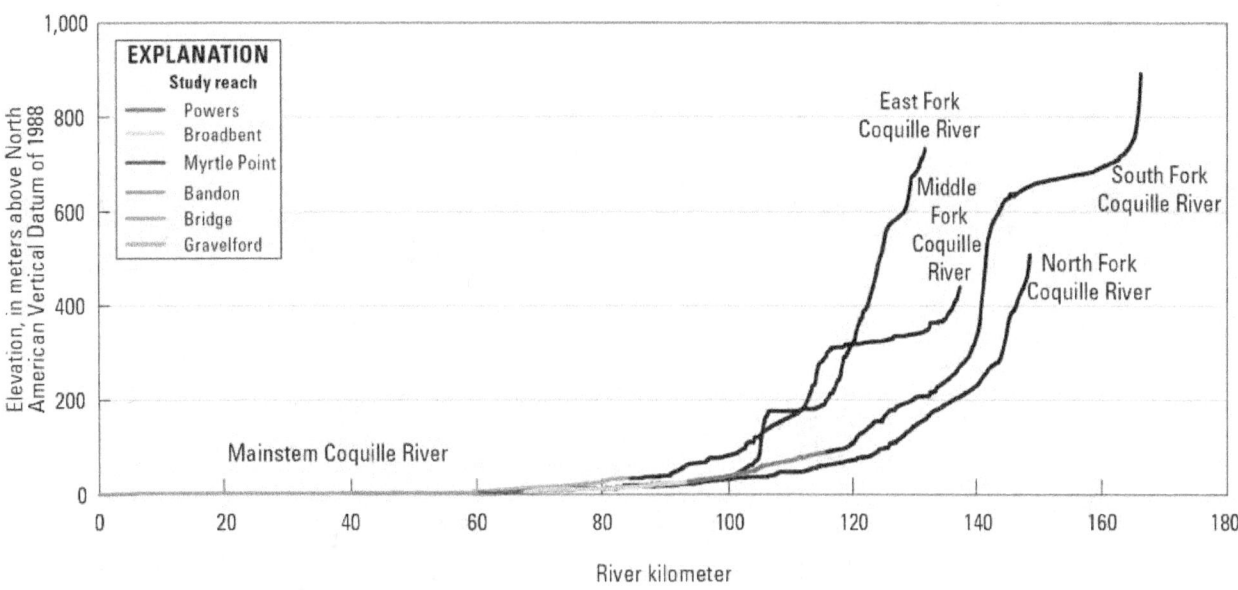

Figure 2. Graph showing the longitudinal profile of the Coquille River basin, southwestern Oregon, as determined from the U.S. Geological Survey 10-m Digital Elevation Model (DEM).

South Fork Coquille River upstream of Rock Creek

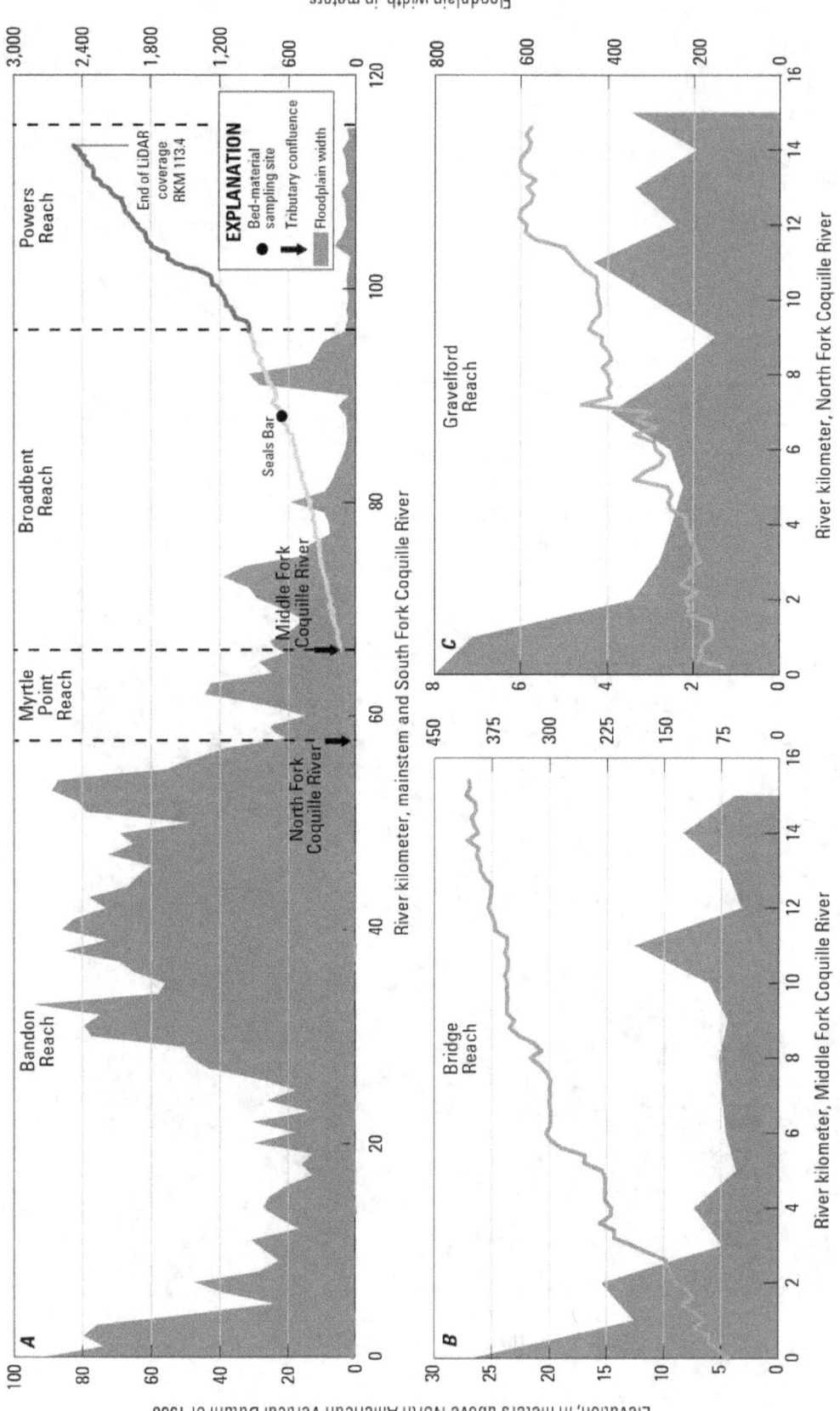

Figure 3. Graphs showing longitudinal profiles and floodplain widths for the (A) Powers, Broadbent, Myrtle Point, and Bandon Reaches on the mainstem and South Fork Coquille River, (B) Bridge Reach on the Middle Fork Coquille River, and (C) Gravelford Reach on the North Fork Coquille River, southwestern Oregon. Elevations were derived from the 1-m Light Detection And Ranging (LiDAR) topographic survey and floodplain widths were derived from LiDAR, soils and geology maps, and aerial photographs.

Table 1. Summary of U.S. Geological Survey (USGS) streamflow-gaging station information for the Coquille River basin, southwestern Oregon.

[Station ID, USGS gaging station number; ~, approximately; km; kilometer; RKM, river kilometer; km^2, square kilometer; WY, water year; m^3/s, cubic meter per second; --, data not available]

Station name	Station ID	Study reach	Location	Drainage area (km²)	Period of record (WY)	Mean annual flow (m3/s)	Peak flow (m3/s)	Date of peak flow
South Fork Coquille River above Panther Creek near Illahae	14324600	--	~28.2 km upstream of study area	81	1957–70	4.1	250	12/22/1964
South Fork Coquille River near Illahae	14324700	--	~22.6 km upstream of study area	105	1957–74	5.6	340	12/22/1964
South Fork Coquille River near Powers	14324900	--	~8.5 km upstream of study area	241	1957–70	14.6	838	12/22/1964
South Fork Coquille River at Powers	14325000	Powers	RKM 105	438	1917–26, 1929– present	22.0	1,385	12/22/1964
Middle Fork Coquille River near Myrtle Point	14326500	Bridge	RKM 3.9	790	1931–46	21.0	668	1/2/1933
North Fork Coquille River near Fairview	14326800	--	~20.1 km upstream of study area	191	1964–81	8.0	220	3/2/1972
North Fork Coquille River near Myrtle Point	14327000	Gravelford	RKM 6.6	730	1929–46, 1964–68	26.1	1,088	12/24/1964

Streamflow in the Coquille River basin follows seasonal precipitation patterns, peaking in winter, when precipitation is the greatest, and receding to baseflow in summer, when precipitation is infrequent. Average annual rainfall varies from 1.14 meters (m) in the Camas Valley (fig. 1) to 3.05 m in the upper South Fork Coquille River basin (Coquille Watershed Association [1997] as cited in Coquille Indian Tribes [2007]). Mean annual flow is 22.0 m^3/s on the South Fork Coquille River at Powers (1917–1926, 1928–2010; table 1). High flows (for example, exceeding 200 m^3/s on the South Fork Coquille River; fig. 4A) are most common from November to March, when rainfall saturates the thin soils in the steeper, high elevation areas of the watershed (fig. 2; Coquille Indian Tribe, 2007). In summer, base flows are sustained by groundwater contributions, but generally recede to less than 1 m^3/s on the South Fork Coquille River (U.S. Geological Survey, 2010). Although the Coquille River is unregulated by any large-scale hydropower projects, hydrologic alterations include withdrawals of surface water for municipal, domestic, and irrigation uses as well as diking and channel straightening in low elevation areas to speed drainage after floods (Coquille Indian Tribe, 2007).

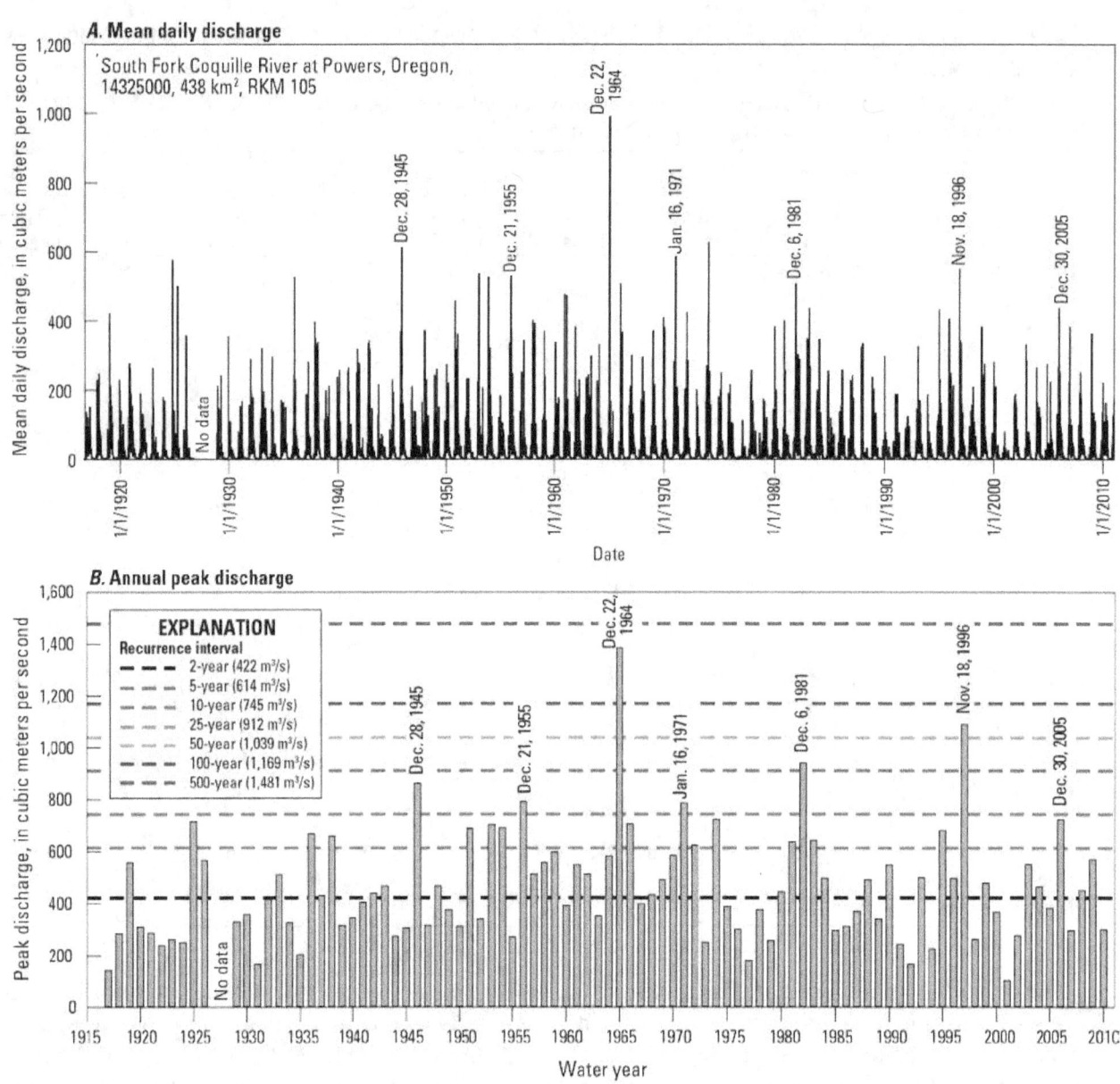

Figure 4. Graphs showing (A) mean daily discharge and (B) annual peak discharge for the U.S. Geological Survey streamflow-gaging station at Powers (14325000) on the South Fork Coquille River, southwestern Oregon. Flow recurrence intervals from Cooper (2005).

Because the delivery and transport of bed material in the Coquille River basin are driven in part by high flows, we identified peak flows from gaging station streamflow records. Peaks of record were 1,088 m^3/s on December 24, 1964, for the lower North Fork Coquille River near Myrtle Point (14327000) and 668 m^3/s on January 2, 1933, for the Middle Fork Coquille River near Myrtle Point (14326500; table 1). The 1964 flood

is also the peak of record on the South Fork Coquille River, with streamflow reaching 1,385 m^3/s on December 22, 1964, exceeding the current estimate of a 100-year recurrence-interval event (table 1; fig. 4B). Prior to 1964, flows on the South Fork Coquille River exceeded a 10-year event on December 28, 1945, and December 21, 1955 (fig. 4B). Since 1964, peak flows on the South Fork Coquille River have exceeded a 25-

year event on December 9, 1981, and a 50-year event on November 18, 1996 (fig. 4B).

Historical large floods in the Coquille River basin occurred in 1861, 1881, and 1890 (Benner, 1991). Although no data are available to compare the magnitudes of these and more recent floods, the 1861 flood shifted the location of the Coquille River mouth, and the 1890 flood triggered a large landslide on Salmon Creek, a tributary joining the South Fork Coquille River near RKM 107. Dodge (1898) provides the following description of the 1890 event:

> "A journey up the small stream [Salmon Creek] in the summer time reveals wonderful scenery. For a distance of four miles a tortuous channel has been worn through rocks and steep declivities about one hundred rods wide, excepting a few narrow gorges, and the bottom of this channel is paved with rocks, sand and gravel, with occasional clusters of boulders that weigh tons, and yet the torrents of winter roll them from place to place, changing the surface of the bed of the stream at each season according to the volume of water. Four miles from the mouth of the canyon a wonderful slide took place in 1890, when the side of a mountain literally broke loose and went down several hundred feet with its massive trees and rocks and built a dam across Salmon creek seventy-five feet high, forming what has since been known as Salmon Lake in a narrow valley above, but with-in a few days the dam gave way and the timber, debris and mass of earth that formed the dam was swept down the stream and where the junction was made with the main river it raised the stream twenty-five feet almost in the twinkling of an eye, and as the flood swept onward the farmers could not understand why the sudden rise had taken place. At Wm. H. Harris' place and the Hermann homestead, the river raised twelve feet in a few minutes and trees two or three hundred feet long were so thick for a mile up and down the river that one could have crossed the stream easily at any point on the drift-

wood. At Myrtle Point the large bridge came near being torn out, and it was said that one could have walked on the timber in the river from the town to Rackleff's mill. The massive pile of timber was stopped at Coquille City by J. A. Lyons' boom, and for a mile above the town trees piled up and formed a gorge that took days to loosen and open the river to navigation."

This account of the 1890 flood by Dodge captures the substantial contributions of wood and sediment into the Coquille River network by mass movements and the ability of the South Fork Coquille River to transport sediment and wood nearly 68 km from its confluence with Salmon Creek to the town of Coquille.

Historical Channel Descriptions

As indicated by the above description of the effects of the 1890 flood on Salmon Creek and the South Fork and mainstem Coquille River, historical observations of river channels are useful reference points for comparing present channel conditions. Many of the relevant historical observations of channels in the Coquille River basin address interactions between the channel, large wood, and sediment accumulation and erosion, chiefly in relation to navigation and local timber industry practices. In particular, Benner (1991) documented and summarized the importance of large wood in the Coquille River basin prior to substantial Euro-American development in the late 1800s. Other accounts such as those by the Corps of Engineers (1891), also describe wood transport in the Coquille River system:

> "The various forks of the Coquille drain densely timbered territory, and at every freshet many trees, stumps, etc., are brought down. Some of these lodge at different points, forming isolated snags, or are grouped together into jams. These snags and jams, in turn, induce the formation of shoals of sand and gravel."

More detailed accounts by the Corps of Engineers describe conditions along the lower

Coquille River in the section of primary interest for navigation. From RKM 39.6 near the town of Coquille to the mouth, "the river is described as presenting the features of a natural canal, its banks steep, its channel free from rocks, shoals, or rapids, and obstructed only by a few snags, easily to be removed" (U.S. Army Corps of Engineers, 1879).

Farther downstream, the Coquille River had extensive accumulations of driftwood at its mouth in the 1800s as indicated on maps produced by the Corps of Engineers (Benner, 1991). Reports by the Corps of Engineers also highlight the shifting position of the channel and shoaling at the river's mouth (U.S. Army Corps of Engineers, 1879). Assistant Engineer Channing Bolton stated:

> "The difficulty here, as at Coos Bay, seems to be the shifting sands and crooked channel, together with the addition of a much narrower entrance, and that obstructed by many dangerous rocks. Captain Parker, owner of the tug and pilot at the mouth of the river, informed me that the sands are so shifting that he cannot rely on information gained one day for the next, but has to make a thorough examination of the channel before each trip."

Additionally, these reports by the Corps of Engineers (1879) suggest that the position of the Coquille River mouth likely shifted seasonally:

> "…sand driven along by the strong northwest winds in summer rapidly prolongs this north spit, and that the current on the ebb, in the dry season, is spread over too great an area to give it sufficient scouring force to carry these sands out to deep water; the channel is therefore pushed down through the rocks until it occupies its present position. As soon as the southwest gales commence in the winter the formation of the spit ceases, and the current of the river, greatly increased by freshets from heavy rains, strikes it almost directly a short distance below the rocky ledge and forces a channel through it, thus entirely

avoiding the rocks below, near the present entrance."

Other historical accounts highlight the dynamic nature of the channels in upper portions of the basin. In *Pioneer History of Coos and Curry Counties*, Orvil Dodge (1898) described changes in channel position, streamflow, and tide relevant to trade and navigation in the basin. In the following quotation, Dodge indicated changes in the location of the South Fork Coquille River channel near the town of Norway (RKM 55.6; fig. 1):

> "Soon after Reed and Nelson started trade at Norway, Asa Myers and Mr. Hoover arrived from the east and erected a saw mill in 1876 and in 1880 a flouring mill on the south side of the stream. They made excellent flour and good lumber, but the channel of the stream changed in a few years leaving the mill so far from the river that it was too expensive to get logs from the water to the mill."

Farther upstream near the confluence of the South and Middle Forks of the Coquille River (RKM 66.2), Dodge described channel aggradation (resulting in a loss of tidal prism) and widening:

> "Those pioneers now distinctly remember that the tide raised at least two feet at the junction of the Middle and South forks, but since civilization has set in with its march of progress in cultivating the soil, the river has widened and filled up so that the tides are only perceptible at Myrtle Point, two miles below the confluence of those two arms of the river at full moon tide."

In another account, Dodge depicted channel aggradation and bank erosion also near the confluence of the South and Middle Forks of the Coquille River:

> "Hoffman established a ferry across the two rivers, and for twenty years it was a lucrative business, but the stream has filled with debris so that fords are now plentiful. Tide water raised at this place and swelled the stream two or three feet in depth, until the farmer

cleared the timber from the banks and thus left them at the mercy of the angry torrents in the winter, and the banks soon caved and found the bed of the stream, and now the mighty ocean fails to send her floods within three or four miles of the place they reached before civilization planted her feet on the shores of the stream."

Combined, these historical descriptions indicate that the Coquille River system in the late 1800s was undergoing vertical and planform channel changes, likely in response to large floods as well as natural and anthropogenic inputs of wood and sediment. Riparian clearing, forestry practices, and fires (described below), in particular, likely contributed sediment to the river system. Aggradation of channels, buildup of in-channel wood, reduction in tidal extent, shifts in the location of the river mouth, and other issues culminated in active management of the Coquille River system and actions such as dredging, wood (snag) removal, and the construction of jetties at the mouth (described below).

Occupation, Land Use, and Landscape Disturbance

As alluded to in many of the historical observations described above, multiple anthropogenic processes and disturbances have had substantial effects on sediment yield and transport and channel morphology within the Coquille River basin. Logging, dredging, and mining (gravel and mineral) are human activities that directly affected channel conditions. Fire and mass movements are natural processes affecting sediment yield and transport, but both processes have likely been altered by human activities.

Settlement and Ownership

Several Native American tribes, such as the Coos and Upper Coquille Indian Tribes, inhabited the Coquille River basin prior to Euro-American settlement (Coquille Indian Tribe, 2007). In the 1850s, however, Euro-American settlement began, initially focusing on beaver fur trading and

then expanding to fisheries, agriculture, forestry, and other uses in subsequent years (Coquille Indian Tribe, 2007). Today, approximately 40 percent of the Coquille River basin is privately managed for industrial forestry (Coquille Indian Tribe, 2007). Private lands used for nonindustrial purposes as well as Federal, State, and county lands managed by entities including the Bureau of Land Management (BLM), U.S. Forest Service (USFS), and Coquille Indian Tribe each make up approximately 30 percent of the basin (Coquille Indian Tribe, 2007).

Logging and Splash Damming

Since approximately the 1850s, forests in the Coquille River basin have been logged. The first mill was constructed in 1853 along the lower Coquille River near the town of Bullards (Coos Historical and Maritime Museum, 2011a). Subsequent mills followed, such as the Moore Lumber Company, which began work in Bandon in 1900 and remained a major employer until the 1960s (Coos Historical and Maritime Museum, 2011b). Despite the long history of logging in the basin, we found little data summarizing historical logging volumes and practices. Peck and Park (2006) summarized logging-related activities in the upper portions of the South Fork Coquille River watershed by decade from 1930 to 2000. They reported that logging-related activities have affected approximately 90 km^2 in the upper South Fork Coquille River watershed from 1930 to 2000, with logging activities peaking in the 1960s and 1970s (Peck and Park, 2006).

The tributaries and rivers of the Coquille River basin served as transportation routes (fig. 5A) connecting the upland logging areas with the lowland mills. Initially, channels were cleared of wood and boulders and logs were then floated downstream on the South Fork Coquille River below Powers, mainstem Coquille River, North Fork Coquille River, Middle Fork Coquille River, and numerous tributaries (Benner, 1991; Miller, 2010). The South Fork Coquille River was used for these log drives until about 1914 (Farnell,

Figure 5. Historical photographs showing: (A) a 200-m-long jam of about 5,400 logs near Prosper, Oregon (near river kilometer 7) in 1907, and (B) splash damming on Middle Creek, a tributary to the North Fork Coquille River, in 1912. (A) and (B) used by permission of Roxann Gess Smith of Salem, Oregon, and Stephen Beckham of Portland, Oregon, respectively.

1979). Starting in about 1911, however, instream log transport was enhanced by the use of splash dams (temporary wooden dams used to raise the water level in streams to float logs downstream to sawmills; fig. 5B) to create repeatable and managed floods, which could transport more logs faster (Benner, 1991). In conjunction with the splash dams, the Port of Coquille Commission and other entities cleared riparian vegetation and continued removing wood and boulders from areas downstream of splash dams on the forks of the Coquille River to maximize log transport efficiency (Benner, 1991). About 25 splash dams were operated in the Coquille River basin and located on the North, East, and Middle Forks of the Coquille River and several tributaries, such as Dement Creek on the South Fork Coquille River as well as Myrtle, Rock, Big, and Sandy Creeks on the Middle Fork Coquille River (Benner, 1991). Splash damming was banned by the Oregon State Legislature in 1957 (Phelps, 2011) after a series of court cases citing the deleterious effects of splash damming on riparian properties and bank stability (Benner, 1991).

Splash damming likely has had long-term effects on channels in the Coquille River basin as suggested by Miller (2010) for streams with a history of splash damming along the Oregon coast.

Splash damming in the Coquille River basin likely increased the frequency and magnitude of peak floods and associated flux of sediments within the river network and scouring of the channel bed (possibly to bedrock) As an example, in Camp Creek and West Fork Millicoma River to the north of the Coquille River basin, Phelps (2011) estimated that flows resulting from splash damming likely exceeded 100-year flood events in headwater areas and were comparable to 100-year flood events in downstream areas.

Other alterations to maximize splash dam efficiency, such as blasting of boulders and removal of in-channel wood and riparian vegetation, also contributed to reducing channel complexity while increasing sediment flux and bank instability (Benner, 1991). Since all of the gages operated by the USGS on the South Fork Coquille River were upstream of splash damming activities on Dement Creek (fig. 1), peak flow data from those gaging stations are not useful for identifying flow magnitudes related to splash damming on the South Fork Coquille River. Over time, sediment loads and channel conditions in the basin have likely been influenced by the effects of direct channel manipulations associated with log drives and splash dams as well as by sediment introduced by the subsequent development of logging road networks (Reid and Dunne, 1984; Furniss and others, 1991).

Dredging and Wood Removal for Navigation

As waterways were historically the primary means of transporting goods and materials in the Coquille River basin, economic development in the basin depended on maintaining navigable channels. At the Coquille River mouth, the Corps of Engineers has constructed and maintained jet-

ties and dredged since 1880 (Willingham, 1983). Historical and ongoing dredging has focused on maintaining a stable channel elevation between the jetties and along the lower 2 km of the main-stem Coquille River. Between 1986 and 2010, more than 533,000 m^3 of sediment (primarily sand) was removed from the lower 2 km of the Coquille River, averaging nearly 22,150 m^3 per year (fig. 6).

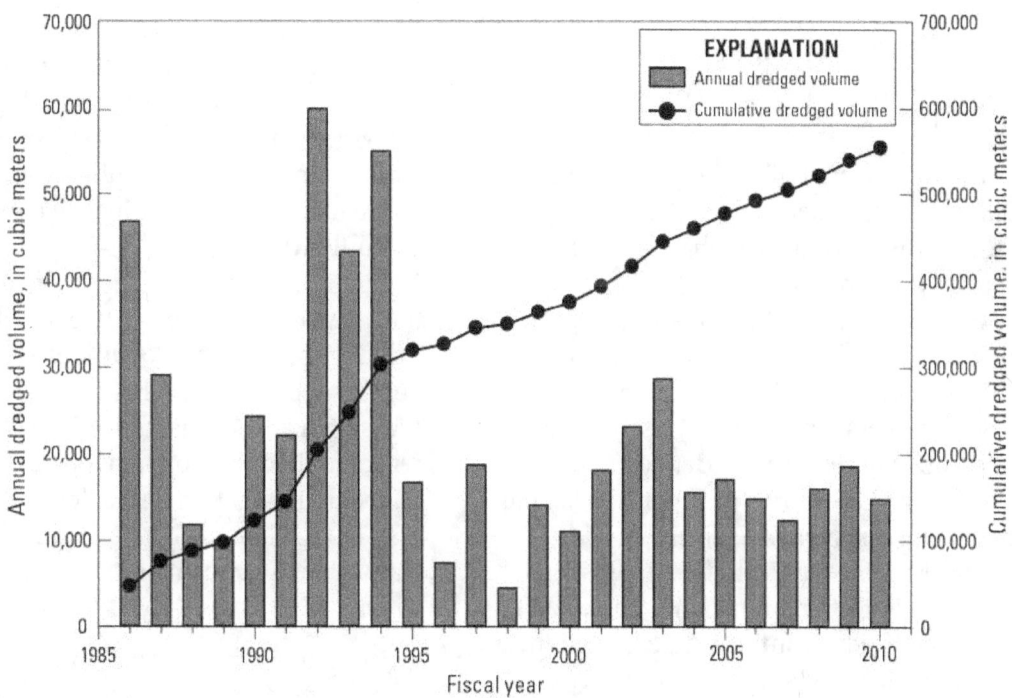

Figure 6. Graph showing reported annual and cumulative volumes of sediment removed from 1986 to 2010 near the mouth of the Coquille River, southwestern Oregon. Data from Judy Linton and Katharine Groth (U.S. Army Corps of Engineers, written commun., 2011) and U.S. Army Corps of Engineers (2010). Fiscal year refers to the Federal fiscal year of October 1 to September 30.

Upriver from the mouth, however, maintaining a navigable channel proved to be more challenging. Early reports described the mainstem river from the towns of Coquille to Norway as "navigable at all seasons of the year," with steamers traveling 60 km upriver to Myrtle Point without the assistance of any channel dredging (quote from the General Land Office Survey of the Coquille River, as cited in Benner, 1991). By 1886, however, steamers had difficulty completing the last mile to Myrtle Point, which prompted the Corps of Engineers to begin scraping bars and removing snags from Coquille to Myrtle Point in 1889 (Benner, 1991). Reports by the Corps of Engineers indicate that some of these shoals consisted of gravel and sand (U.S. Army Corps of Engineers, 1898; Benner, 1991).

In 1889, the Corps of Engineers removed over 22,500 m^3 of material from these shoals. In 1902, the Corps of Engineers abandoned their efforts (except for periodic snagging) between Coquille and Myrtle Point owing to the failure of dredging and pile dikes to maintain a navigable channel (Benner, 1991). From 1889 to 1917, the Corps of Engineers removed 6,748 snags along the river from Myrtle Point to Bandon (Benner, 1991). After the U.S. Corps of Engineers ceased regular channel maintenance upstream of Coquille at RKM 39.6, the Port of Coquille was established in 1911 to maintain the channel in this upper section of tidally influenced channel; their activities included dredging approximately 272,000 m^3 and removing 1,890 snags in the 7.2 km of channel near Myrtle Point from 1915 to 1923 (Benner, 1991).

Farther downstream, from Coquille to Bandon, channel sedimentation appears to have increased during the early 1900s. Shoals were absent from the Coquille River from 1889 to 1902, when the Corps of Engineers dredged the channel from Coquille to Myrtle Point (Benner, 1991). By 1910, six shoals had formed in the main channel from Coquille to Bandon, leading to repeated dredging of the channel and removal

of more than 262,300 m^3 of material from 1912 to 1924 (Benner, 1991).

In total, from 1889 to 1924, nearly 557,000 m^3 of sediment was removed from the South Fork and mainstem Coquille River to maintain a navigable channel (from estimates presented in Benner, 1991). From her review of navigation maintenance records, Benner (1991) concluded, "The depth and dredging history of the tidal segment of the Coquille River suggests that the channel water depth has decreased since the time of Euro-American settlement of the area in the 1850s" (pg. 14 of Executive Summary). Material filling the channel was likely derived from logging activities in the headwaters of the basin and splash damming as well as landslides (Florsheim and Williams, 1996). Channel aggradation may partially explain the approximately 3-km reduction in tidal influence on the South Fork Coquille River since Euro-American settlement (Benner, 1991) with the head of tide moving downstream from the confluence of the South and Middle Forks of the Coquille River near RKM 66.2 to approximately RKM 63.2 (Farnell, 1979). Florsheim and Williams (1996) suggested that repeated dredging to maintain water depths conducive to navigation on the lower Coquille River may have initiated channel head cutting and incision farther upstream on the South Fork Coquille River.

Although the rate and type of sediment delivered to the South Fork and mainstem Coquille River have likely been affected by historical land-use practices, the locus of deposition near Myrtle Point reflects the marked reduction in gradient at about RKM 60 (fig. 3A). This gradient discontinuity, in turn, reflects the long-term filling of the tidally affected portion of the lower Coquille River with sediment as a result of Holocene sea-level rise. If sea level stabilizes, then ongoing sedimentation will eventually produce a continuous stream gradient profile to the mouth of the Coquille River as the locus of deposition shifts downstream.

Instream Gravel Mining

Instream gravel mining can potentially result in channel incision and bar armoring (Kondolf, 1994). As indicated in a July 31, 1928, article by the Coos Bay Times, gravel has been mined from bars along the South Fork Coquille River to make concrete and support construction needs since at least the 1920s. In 1928, the McGeorge Gravel Company supplied approximately 32,000 m³ of material for the Coos Bay-Roseburg and Roosevelt Coast highways (now U.S. Highway 101); this material was mined from the South Fork Coquille River near the town of Gaylord (RKM 98.4; fig. 7) using railroad cars, conveyor belts, and other machinery (Coos Bay Times, 1928). A compilation of mines by the Oregon Department of Geology and Mineral Industries (DOGAMI) indicates the approximate locations of 54 mines for sand and gravel along the channels and floodplains of the mainstem, forks, and tributaries of the Coquille River; a majority of these historical sites are concentrated within or adjacent to the Coquille River study area (Oregon Department of Geology and Mineral Resources, 1999). As of 2011, six instream mining permits with a cumulative annual removal limit of approximately 76,400 m³ from multiple sites on the South Fork Coquille River are on file with the Corps of Engineers and Oregon Department of State Lands (Judy Linton, U.S. Army Corps of Engineers, written commun., 2010; Robert Lobdell, Oregon Department of State Lands, written commun., 2011). See the "Gravel-Operator Information and Surveys" section for more details on instream gravel mining in the Coquille River study area.

Mineral Mining

Like other rivers along the Oregon coast, the Coquille River basin has a history of gold and other mineral mining. In 1853, gold was discovered slightly north of the Coquille River mouth at Whiskey Run Beach (fig. 1; Coos Historical and Maritime Museum, 2011a). Miners also found gold in Johnson and Salmon Creeks, two trib-

Figure 7. Historical photograph from a Coos Bay Times (1928) article showing the McGeorge Gravel Company's mining site on the South Fork Coquille River near Gaylord, Oregon. Dolores Knight of the Coos Bay Public Library provided this copy of the photograph.

utaries to the South Fork Coquille River (fig. 1), in 1854 and 1860, respectively (Dodge, 1898). Based on historical mining practices in other coastal basins like the Umpqua River basin (Beckham, 1986), placer deposits along the South Fork Coquille River and its tributaries may have been mined hydraulically, potentially liberating large volumes of sediment from streamside terraces. Other mineral mining in the basin includes historical coal mining in the lower Coquille River near Beaver Slough and Riverton (Coos Historical and Maritime Museum, 2011a). Today, recreational, small-scale suction dredging occurs primarily in the Johnson Creek basin and, to a lesser extent, along the South Fork Coquille River (Oregon Department of Environmental Quality, 2000).

Fire

Since Euro-American settlement, the Coquille River basin has experienced fewer widespread forest fires than the neighboring Rogue and Coos River basins. In 1868, a large fire burned much of the western portion of the Coos River basin, north of the Coquille River, with a small portion of the fire affecting the lower Coquille estuary. In 1889, a fire burned the Salmon Creek watershed, which preceded the 1890 flood that triggered a large slide and ensuing debris flow on Salmon Creek and South Fork and mainstem Coquille River (Dodge, 1898; as described in the "Hydrology" section above). Small wildfires have been noted along the East Fork Coquille River during the latter half of the 19th century (Zybach, 2003). Later, in the summer of 1936, a heat wave accompanied by low humidity caused many small fires to break out in Coos County, with the most notable being the Bear Creek Fire (approximately 590 km^2) that completely destroyed the town of Bandon (Douthit, 1981). Subsequent fires have affected small (7.5 km^2 or less) areas of the watershed (Peck and Park, 2006; U.S. Forest Service, 2008; Oregon Partnership for Disaster Resilience, 2010).

Mass Movements

As described by Dodge (1898), landslides and debris flows have probably always been a substantial source of sediment to the steep and rain-soaked Coquille River basin. In particular, formations such as the Tyee, Flournoy, and Lookingglass in the sedimentary subdivision of the Coast Range geologic province are susceptible to mass movements and debris flows (Lane, 1987; Burns, 1998; Roering and others, 2005). The serpentinite rocks within the Klamath Mountains geologic province are also susceptible to mass movements, but make up less than 1 percent of the basin (Oregon Department of Environmental Quality, 2000; Ma and others, 2009). Mass wasting is also more prevalent near faults and at the contacts between units where the bedding has greater dip angles (Lane, 1987). Mass movements are also affected by human activities, chiefly road construction and clear cutting associated with timber harvest (Swanson and Dyrness, 1975; Beschta, 1978; Amaranthus and others, 1985; Harden and others, 1995). For example, of the 80 landslides in the Rock and Johnson Creek watersheds (within the South Fork Coquille River basin), about 40 were apparently related to logging or road construction (Oregon Department of

Environmental Quality, 2000; Ma and others, 2009). In the portions of the watershed underlain by the relatively hard rocks of the Klamath Mountains geologic province, mass movements probably are a substantial contributor of coarse bed material to downstream river sections. In the areas underlain by other Coast Range sedimentary and volcanic rocks, mass movements likely contribute more fine sediment loads as larger clasts quickly abrade into smaller particles (Jones and others, 2010; Mangano and others, 2011).

Study Area

For the purposes of this assessment, the overall geography, geomorphology, and land-use history of the Coquille River basin led to delineation of a focused study area, including (1) the South Fork Coquille River from RKM 115.4 near its confluence with Upper Land Creek to RKM 58.5 at its confluence with the North Fork Coquille River, (2) the mainstem Coquille River from RKM 58.5 at the confluence of the South and North Forks of the Coquille River to its mouth, (3) the Middle Fork Coquille River from RKM 15.4 to its confluence with the South Fork Coquille River, and (4) the North Fork Coquille River from RKM 14.6 to its confluence with the South Fork Coquille River (fig. 1). These mainstem and tributary corridors contain most of the alluvial deposits within the basin and have had the most active and historical instream gravel mining. This study area, encompassing 145.4 km of river channel in total, was further subdivided into six reaches based on topography and hydrology (figs. 1 and 3A–C; tables 2 and 3).

Landslide on the South Fork Coquille River upstream of China Flat Bar

Table 2. Summary of characteristics for study reaches on the South Fork and mainstem of the Coquille River, southwestern Oregon

[RKM, river kilometer; km², square kilometers; m, meter]

River reach characteristic	Mainstem Coquille River	South Fork Coquille River		
	Bandon Reach	Myrtle Point Reach	Broadbent Reach	Powers Reach
RKM	58.5-0	66.2–58.5	96.9–66.2	115.4–96.9
Reach and channel description	Entire reach tidally affected; unconfined channel composed of alluvium; jetties stabilize location of river mouth; intermittent bars; larger tidal bars in lower 15 km	Tidally affected to RKM 63.2; channel composed of alluvium with localized confinements; bars throughout reach	Channel mostly alluvium and alternates between unconfined and confined segments with some bedrock in channel and banks; tall, nearly vertical banks in several locations; bars throughout reach	Channel alternates between alluvium and bedrock and unconfined and confined segments; higher-gradient, confined segments dominated by boulders and cascades; bars throughout reach
Drainage area at up- and downstream boundaries[1] (km²)	2,284–2,745	1,437–1,536	487–637	339–487
Reach gradient[2] (m/m)	0.00002	0.00040	0.00090	0.00270
Major flow factors	Water withdrawals for municipal, domestic, and irrigation uses	Same as Bandon Reach	Same as Bandon Reach	Same as Bandon Reach
Background sedimentation drivers	Low-gradient promotes deposition of bed and suspended loads from upstream sources	Same as Bandon Reach	Inputs from tributaries, upstream sources, and eroded bank material	Inputs from tributaries and other upstream sources such as eroded bank material, debris flows, and landslides
Channel disturbance factors	Same as Myrtle Point Reach plus jetty construction and splash damming on tributary; ongoing dredging	Historical dredging; channel straightening and diking; log drives and wood removal; pile dikes; likely historical gravel extraction; upland logging	Log drives, wood removal on mainstem; splash damming, log drives, wood removal on Dement Creek; channel straightening, diking; pile dikes; historical and ongoing instream gravel mining; upland logging	Historical placer (possible hydraulic) mining; ongoing suction dredge mining; log drives, wood removal, boulder blasting; upland logging; historical gravel mining on main stem and tributaries
General channel trends	Alluvium; potential for lateral and vertical channel adjustments	Same as Bandon Reach	Mostly alluvium with some bedrock; substantial lateral channel shifting in unconfined sections; potential for lateral and vertical adjustments	Mixed bed of alluvium and bedrock; some potential for lateral and vertical channel adjustments

[1] Drainage area determined using StreamStats, *http://water.usgs.gov/osw/streamstats/oregon.html*

[2] Reach water-surface gradient determined from 1-m LiDAR DEM available for the entire study area except RKM 115.4–113.4 on the South Fork Coquille River

Table 3. Summary of characteristics for study reaches on the Middle and North Forks of the Coquille River, southwestern Oregon.

[RKM, river kilometer; km^2, square kilometers; m, meter]

River reach characteristics	Middle Fork Coquille River	North Fork Coquille River
	Bridge Reach	Gravelford Reach
RKM	15.4–0	14.6–0
Reach and channel description	Relatively confined channel flowing over mixed bed of bedrock, boulders, and alluvium; bars intermittent in reach	Tidally affected to RKM 0.9; relatively confined channel flows over sand and clay and between muddy banks; bars intermittent in reach
Drainage area at up- and downstream boundaries[1] (km^2)	484–798	712–749
Reach gradient[2] (m/m)	0.0015	0.0003
Major flow factors	Water withdrawals for municipal, domestic, and irrigation uses	Same as Bridge Reach
Background sedimentation drivers	Inputs from tributaries and other upstream sources such as eroded bank material, debris flows, and landslides	Low-gradient promotes deposition of bed and suspended loads from upstream sources
Channel disturbance factors	Splash dams and log drives on mainstem and several tributaries; wood removal; upland logging	Same as Bridge Reach
General channel trends	Flows on a mixed bed of alluvium and bedrock; potential for lateral and vertical channel adjustments	Flows on sand and firm clay; potential for lateral and vertical channel adjustments

[1] Drainage area determined using StreamStats, *http://water.usgs.gov/osw/streamstats/oregon.html*

[2] Reach water-surface gradient determined from 1-m LiDAR DEM

North Fork Coquille River near Gravelford

Powers Reach

The Powers Reach of the South Fork Coquille River stretches from slightly downstream of Upper Land Creek to slightly upstream of Rowland Creek (RKM 115.4-96.9; fig. 8, table 2). The width of the floodplain in the Powers Reach ranges from approximately 50 to 180 m (fig. 3A). The channel flows over bedrock and alluvial deposits and through unconfined (RKM 115.4–103.6, 100.6–98) and confined (RKM 103.6–100.6, 98–96.9) segments in this high-gradient reach (reach water-surface gradient 0.0026 m/m; fig. 3A).

In the upstream-most unconfined segment (RKM 115.4–103.6), the South Fork Coquille River has a local gradient of 0.0021 m/m (fig. 3A), varies in active channel width from 28 to 95 m (from 2009 ortho-imagery for this and all widths reported in this section), and contains elongated point, lateral, and medial bars, particularly at high-amplitude channel bends. At RKM 103.6, the South Fork Coquille River enters the first confined segment (RKM 103.6–100.6) between Hood and Bingham Mountains, where the gradient of the channel increases (0.0054 m/m; fig. 3A) and the active channel narrows to 19 to 39 m. This confined segment is dominated by cascades and boulders, and contains lateral and point bars predominately in eddies, adjacent to rapids, or as a veneer over bedrock outcrops. Entering the downstream-most unconfined segment (RKM 100.6–98), the channel returns to a gradient of 0.0021 m/m (fig. 3A). Here, the channel alternates between valley walls, but remains relatively narrow (29–32 m in active channel width) and contains lateral and point bars comparatively smaller than those in the upstream unconfined segment. In the downstream-most confined segment (RKM 98–96.9), the channel again increases in gradient (0.0041 m/m; fig. 3A), narrows slightly to an active channel width of 15 to 32 m, with rapids, boulders, and bedrock outcrops in and along the channel. The drainage area of the South Fork Coquille in this reach ranges from 339 to 487 km^2 (table 2).

Broadbent Reach

The Broadbent Reach on the South Fork Coquille starts slightly upstream of Rowland Creek and ends at the confluence of the South and Middle Forks of the Coquille River, where the drainage area of the South Fork Coquille River is 637 km^2 (RKM 96.9–66.2; fig. 9; table 2). Like the Powers Reach, the channel in the Broadbent Reach alternates between unconfined (RKM 96.9–90.2, 89.9–86.8, and 83.2–66.2) and confined (RKM 90.2–89.9, 86.8–83.2) segments with the width of the floodplain approaching 1,200 m in its widest section near the town of Broadbent (fig. 3A; fig. 9). Although bedrock outcrops occur in and along the channel throughout this reach, the channel flows predominantly over alluvial deposits and has a lower gradient (0.0009 m/m; fig. 3A; table 2) compared to the Powers Reach. The active channel varies from 25 to 71 m in width. Generally, the channel in the Broadbent Reach contains more numerous, elongated point and lateral bars in the unconfined segments and less numerous, smaller bars in the confined segments. Exposed, nearly vertical banks are visible in several locations (such as near RKM 79, 77.6, 73.4, and 73) in the 2008 LiDAR survey and 2009 orthophotographs.

In the Broadbent Reach, channel modifications include those related to splash damming on Dement Creek and log drives on the South Fork Coquille River (Benner, 1991; Miller, 2010) as well as rock bank-protection structures, construction of access roads (and likely dikes), and instream gravel mining (Clearwater Biostudies, Inc., 2003). In particular, the channel from RKM 78.4–76.9 and 73.8–72.1 has shifted in position owing to rock bank-protection structures and the November 18, 1996 flood (Clearwater Biostudies, Inc., 2003). As of 2011, at least 14 gravel bars in the Broadbent Reach are sites of permitted instream gravel mining (Judy Linton, U.S. Army Corps of Engineers, written commun., 2010; Robert Lobdell, Oregon Department of State Lands, written commun., 2011).

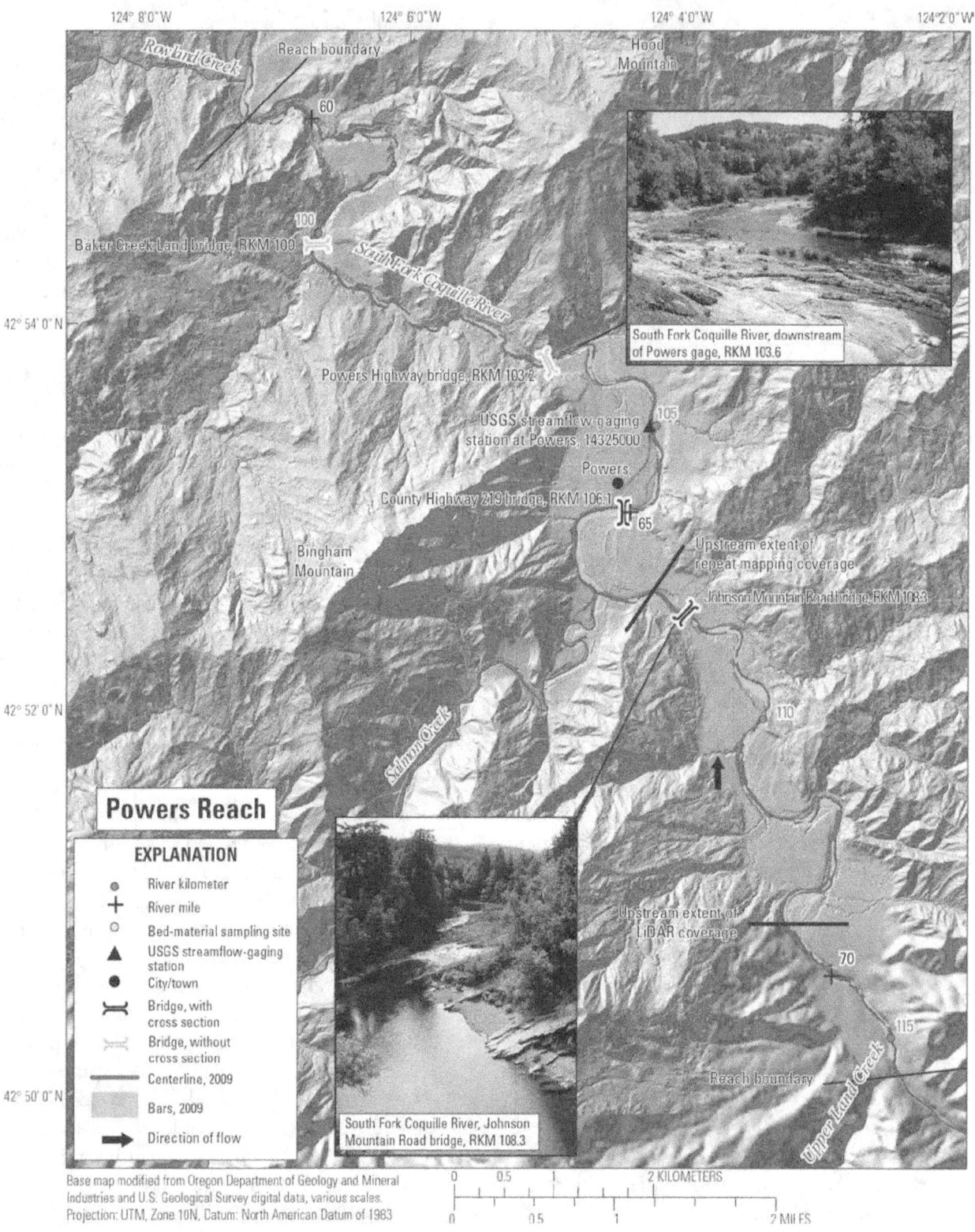

Figure 8. Map showing key locations and bars and channel centerline delineated from 2009 orthophotographs and field reconnaissance photographs for the Powers Reach on the South Fork Coquille River, southwestern Oregon.

22

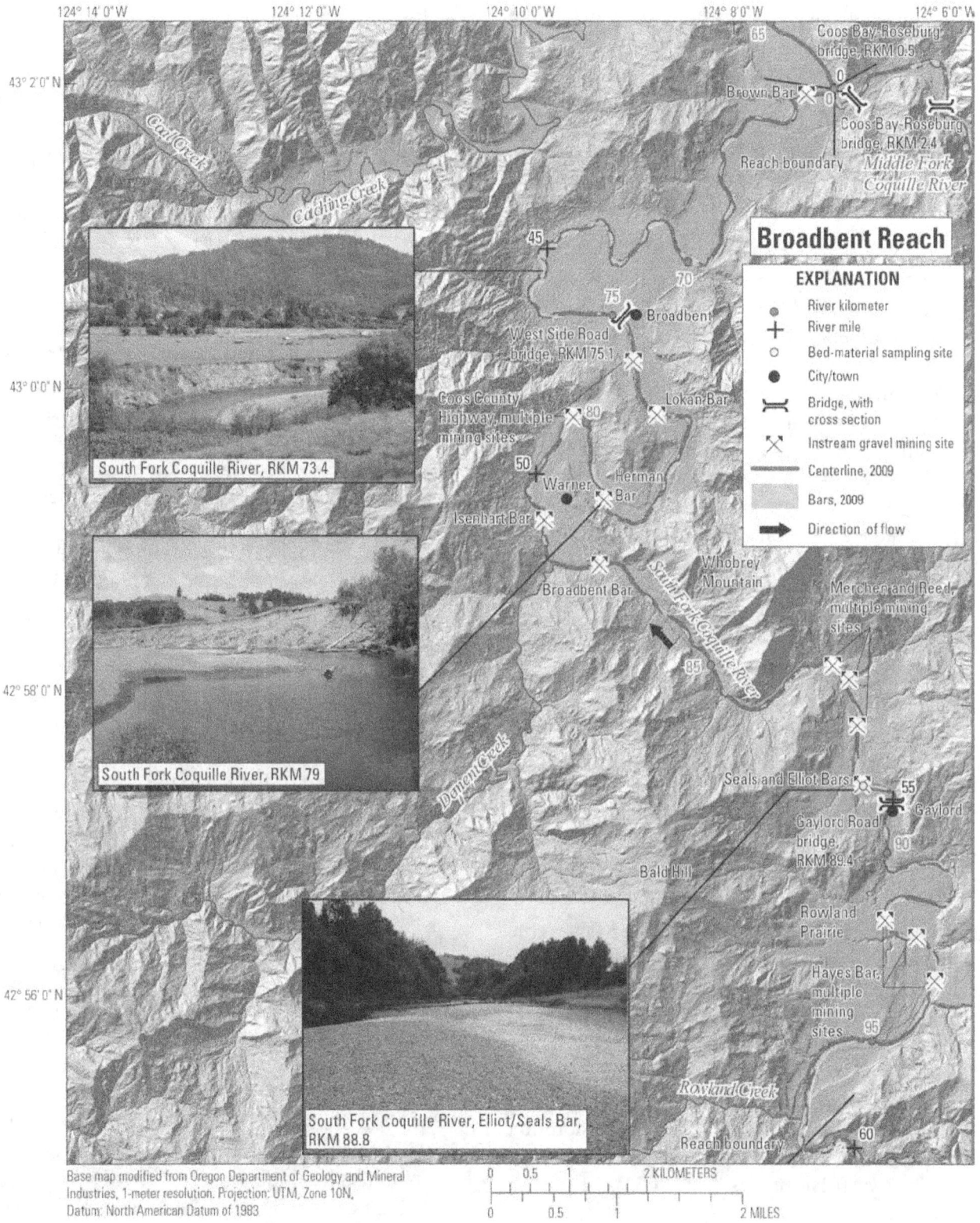

Figure 9. Map showing key locations and bars and channel centerline delineated from 2009 orthophotographs and field reconnaissance photographs for the Broadbent Reach on the South Fork Coquille River, southwestern Oregon.

Additional sites, such as those operated by the McGeorge Gravel Company near Gaylord, were mined historically. Ongoing mitigation efforts aim to increase bank stability and riparian vegetation (Clearwater Biostudies, Inc., 2003; Florsheim and Williams, 1996).

Myrtle Point Reach

The Myrtle Point Reach on the South Fork Coquille River runs from the confluence of the South and Middle Forks of the Coquille River to the confluence of the South and North Forks of the Coquille River (RKM 66.2-58.5; fig. 10). This 7.7-km-long reach spans the transition from fluvial (or river influenced) to tidally influenced, with the lower 4.7 km currently affected by tides. Floodplain width ranges from 450 to 1,330 m (fig. 3A). This low-gradient (0.0004 m/m; fig. 3A, table 2) section of the South Fork Coquille River flowing over alluvium was treated as one distinct reach for the purposes of this study based on tributary inputs and the occurrence of bars throughout the reach even though it contains a mixture of fluvial and tidal environments. Comparison of the aerial photographs used in this study suggests that the active channel is moderately confined in places such as near RKM 66.2–64.8 and 61.4–59.4, owing possibly to dikes and other anthropogenic modifications of the floodplain. The width of the active channel varies from 28 to 62 m. The drainage area of the South Fork Coquille River ranges from 1,437 km^2 at the reach's upstream boundary to 1,536 km^2 at the reach's downstream boundary (table 2). Historically, the Corps of Engineers, Port of Coquille, and other entities removed sediment and wood from the channel, cleared riparian vegetation, and stabilized banks in this reach (Benner, 1991; Farnell, 1979). Like the Broadbent Reach, channel conditions have changed owing to the addition of rock bank protection and road construction (Clearwater Biostudies, Inc., 2003).

Bandon Reach

The tidally influenced Bandon Reach encompasses the entire mainstem Coquille River from the confluence of the South and North Forks to the river's mouth (RKM 58.5–0; fig. 11). The low-gradient channel (0.00002 m/m; fig. 3A, table 2) flows over alluvium with an active channel ranging from 34 to 87 m wide in the reach's upper 32.5 km and from 63 to approximately 1,160 m wide in the reach's lower 26 km. The width of floodplain varies greatly from 380 m near RKM 17 to 2,830 m near RKM 33 (fig. 3A). The floodplain is generally the narrowest from Riverton to where the river enters the coastal Quaternary terraces (fig. 11). Bars are present in the upper 1.2 km of the reach and then are rare until the lowermost 15 km, where bars and tidal flats increase in size as the Coquille River enters the coastal plain. The drainage area of the Coquille River at its mouth is 2,745 km^2. River management actions include the construction and maintenance of jetties at the river's mouth, historical and ongoing dredging to maintain the navigation channel in the lowermost 2 km of the river, and historical dredging and wood removal throughout the reach (Benner, 1991; Willingham, 1983).

Bridge Reach

The Bridge Reach is the only study reach on the Middle Fork Coquille River; it extends from near the town of Bridge to the confluence of the Middle and South Forks of the Coquille River (RKM 15.4–0; fig. 12). Draining a rugged, mountainous area, this section of the Middle Fork Coquille River has a gradient of 0.0015 m/m and step-pool morphology (fig. 3B; table 3). The floodplain is narrow in this reach, ranging from 50 m where the floodplain traverses the Roseburg Formation basalts (part of the volcanic subdivision of the Coast Range geologic province) to 400 m near the confluence with the South Fork Coquille River (fig. 3B). Comprising a mixed bed of bedrock, boulders, and alluvium, the 20–44-m-wide channel is narrow and active. This reach contains intermittent bars (primarily within eddies of high-amplitude bends) that increase in abundance downstream of RKM 3.2. The drainage area of the Middle Fork Coquille River ranges from 484 to 798 km^2 in this reach (table 3).

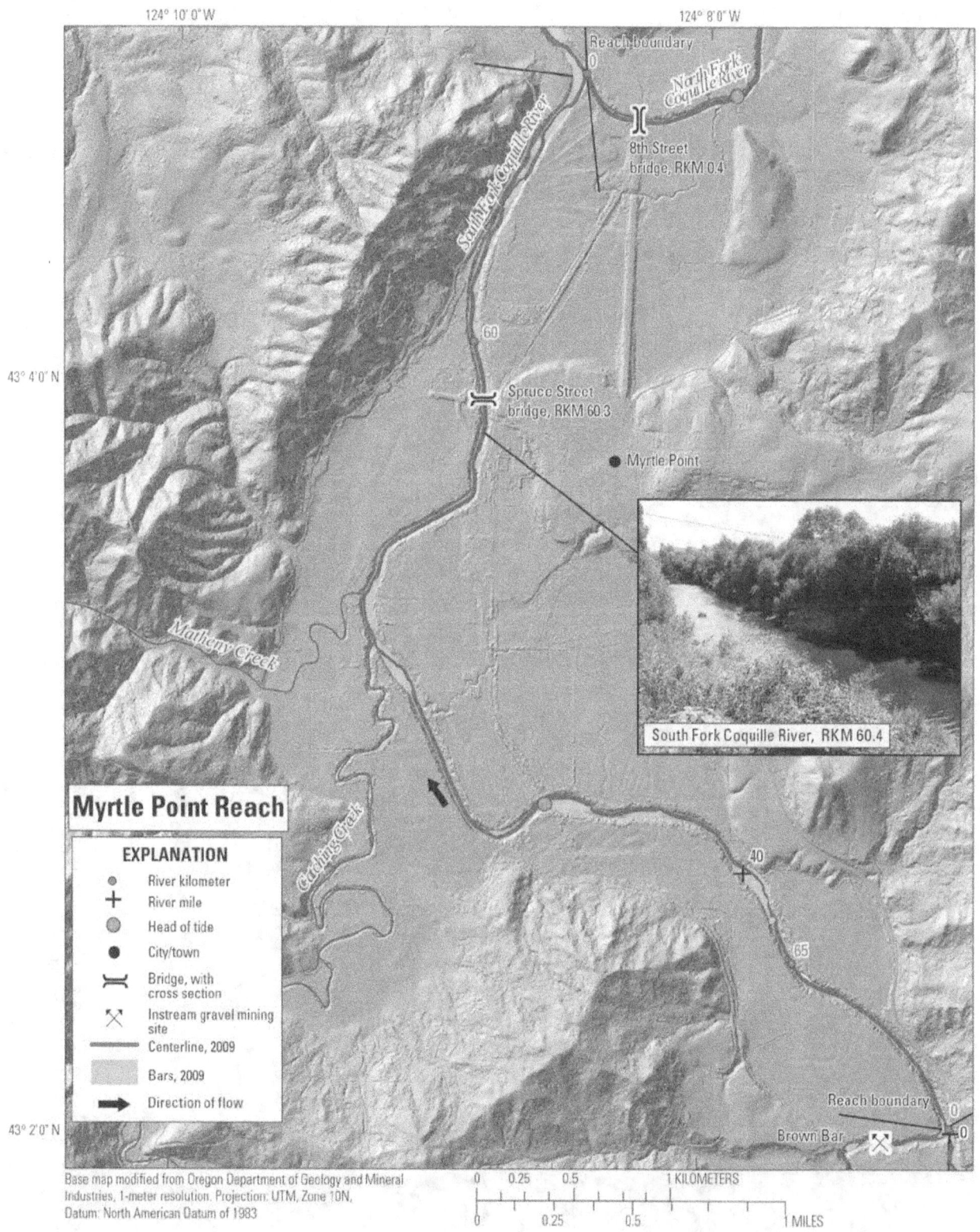

Figure 10. Map showing key locations and bars and channel centerline delineated from 2009 orthophotographs and a field reconnaissance photograph for the Myrtle Point Reach on the South Fork Coquille River, southwestern Oregon.

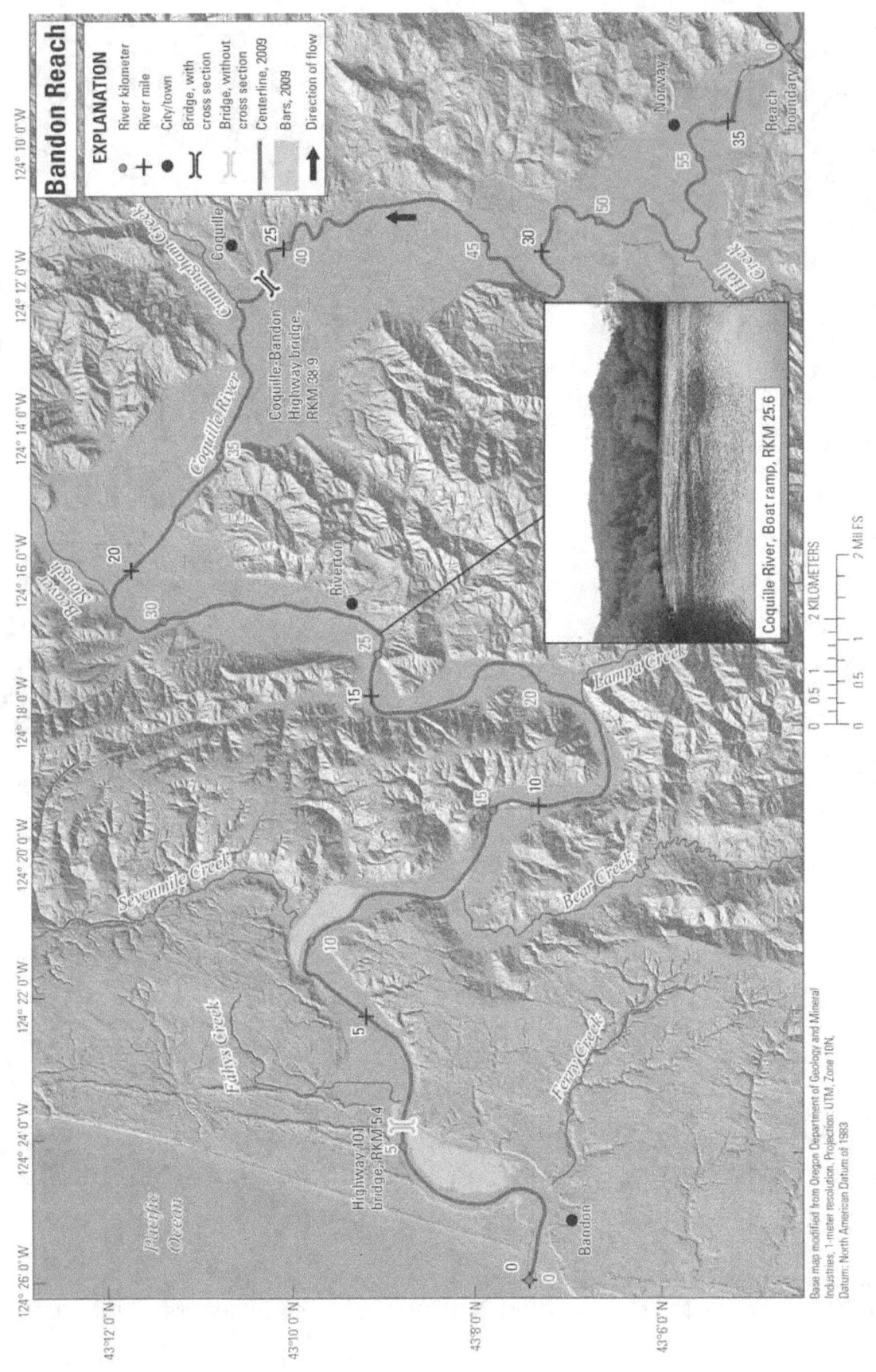

Base map modified from Oregon Department of Geology and Mineral
Industries; 1-meter resolution. Projection: UTM, Zone 10N,
Datum: North American Datum of 1983

Figure 11. Map showing key locations and bars and channel centerline delineated from 2009 orthophotographs and a field reconnaissance photograph for the Bandon Reach on the mainstem Coquille River, southwestern Oregon.

Figure 12. Map showing key locations and bars and channel centerline delineated from 2009 orthophotographs and field reconnaissance photographs for the Bridge Reach on the Middle Fork Coquille River, southwestern Oregon.

Base map modified from Oregon Department of Geology and Mineral Industries, 1-meter resolution. Projection: UTM, Zone 10N. Datum: North American Datum of 1983

The Middle Fork Coquille River accounts for 29.2 percent of the drainage area in the Coquille River basin. Historically, log drives and splash damming occurred on the Middle Fork Coquille River (Farnell, 1979), likely resulting in the removal of in-channel wood and boulders as well as riparian vegetation.

Gravelford Reach

The Gravelford Reach on the North Fork Coquille River encompasses the 14.6-km-long section from near the confluence of the North and East Forks of the Coquille River to the confluence of the North and South Forks of the Coquille River (RKM 14.6–0; fig. 13). This low gradient reach (0.0003 m/m; fig. 3C; table 3) is tidally affected to RKM 0.9. The floodplain varies from 150 to 347 m in width for most of the reach, but then widens to 800 m near the confluence with the South Fork Coquille River (fig. 3C). Flowing over alluvium such as sand and clay in locations (Oregon Department of Transportation, written commun., 2010) and between muddy banks, the active channel is relatively narrow, ranging from 12 to 19 m wide upstream of RKM 6.6, 12 to 23 m wide downstream of RKM 6.6, and up to 48 m wide near the river's mouth. Pile dikes and bank protection structures flank the channel in several locations. The drainage area of the North Fork Coquille River in this reach ranges from 712 to 749 km^2 (table 3). The combined contributing area of the North Fork Coquille River is 27.3 percent of the area in the Coquille River basin. Like the Middle Fork Coquille River, the North Fork Coquille River was subject to log drives and splash damming (Farnell, 1979).

Approach and Key Findings

For this study, we reviewed existing datasets and studies regarding channel condition and bed-material transport in the Coquille River basin, applied reconnaissance-level GIS analyses, and made field observations and particle size measurements in July 2010. The objectives of these efforts were to (1) identify existing datasets that would support more detailed analyses of bed-material transport and channel condition, (2) summarize reported volumes of mined and deposited material at instream gravel mining sites, (3) identify locations where the channel may be aggrading, incising, prone to lateral channel migration, or stable, (4) characterize broad-scale patterns in bar and channel features using photographs spanning 1939–2009, and (5) assess the relations between transport capacity and sediment supply for each study reach. This study provides a preliminary review of channel condition and bed-material transport in the Coquille River basin and identifies outstanding issues relevant to the permitting of instream gravel mining that may be addressed by future studies. The following sections summarize each of the major activities and key findings.

Review of Existing Datasets

We assessed the availability of spatial datasets in the Coquille River basin that could be used to evaluate channel condition and bed-material transport. This search focused primarily on aerial and orthophotographs, but included geospatial datasets, such as LiDAR topographic data, geologic maps, General Land Office surveys, and navigation surveys.

Aerial and Orthophotographs

This study reviewed aerial and orthophotograph coverages of the Coquille River basin available from the Corps of Engineers' Aerial Photograph Library (Portland, Oregon) and the University of Oregon Map and Aerial Photography Library (Eugene, Oregon) as well as digital orthophotographs available from online sources. Other potential sources of photographs not investigated for this review include the Bureau of Land Management, National Archives, county government collections, and private timber companies.

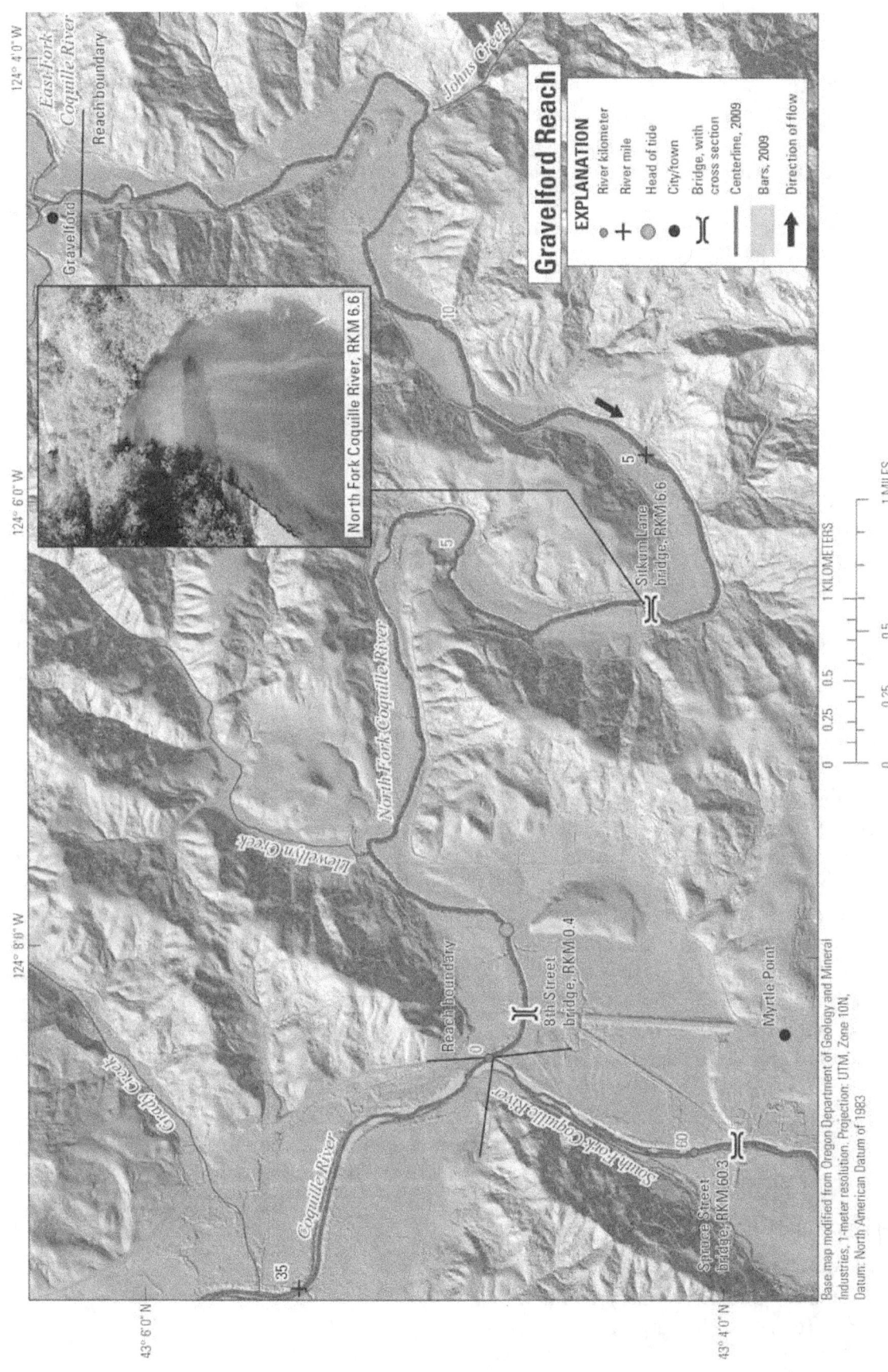

Figure 13. Map showing key locations and bars and channel centerline delineated from 2009 orthophotographs and a field reconnaissance photograph for the Gravelford Reach on the North Fork Coquille River, southwestern Oregon.

At least 11 sets of photographs taken from 1942 to 2011 provide complete coverage of the entire Coquille River study area (table 4). Additional sets of aerial photographs provide coverage of multiple reaches, with the most comprehensive coverages taken in 1939, 1957, 1986, and 1989. The Bandon Reach, particularly in the lowermost section near the coast, was photographed more frequently (table 4). In addition to the aerial photographs listed in table 4, at least 29 sets of aerial photographs of the Coquille River mouth were taken for navigation and jetty maintenance purposes from 1959 to 2002.

Eight photograph sets taken in 1939, 1967, 1989, 1995, 2000–01, 2005, 2009, and 2011 (table 4) provide comprehensive coverage of all or most of the study area and were taken during low flow months at scales of 1:24,000 or greater. These photograph sets would be suitable for use in future studies assessing long-term changes in channel attributes, bar frequency and area, and vegetative cover.

For this study, we used photographs taken in 1939, 1967, 2005, and 2009 for repeat bar and channel delineations (table 4). At the time of this study, the 2009 photographs provided the most recent coverage of the study area. Additionally, we selected the 1939, 1967, and 2005 photographs to enable data comparisons between this study and completed studies on the Chetco (Wallick and others, 2010), Umpqua (Wallick and others, 2011), and Rogue (Jones and others, 2012) Rivers and Hunter Creek (Jones and others, 2011). Additionally, the 1939 photographs are the earliest photographic coverage of the study area (table 4) and the 1967 photographs provide complete coverage of the study area following the December 22, 1964, flood, which exceeded a 100-year flood event on the South Fork Coquille River (table 1; fig. 4B).

Historical Maps and Survey Data

We reviewed historical maps and survey data available for the Coquille River study area from several sources (table 5). The purpose of this re-

view was to identify datasets with information on channel condition, the extent and distribution of gravel bars, and channel morphology and bed elevations that could support assessments of channel change in future studies.

The earliest available surveys of the study reaches on the mainstem Coquille River were conducted by the General Land Office (GLO) from 1857 to 1876 (table 5). As summarized by Atwood (2008), the main purpose of GLO surveys was to establish the Township, Range, and Section lines of the Public Land Survey System (PLSS). In some instances, as in the case for the Coquille River, the channel banks were surveyed during the mapping (typically described as "meandering"), thereby providing an accurate plan-view depiction of channel geometry at the time of survey. Further review of the GLO maps and accompanying surveyor notes would help determine if surveyors also recorded any descriptions of channel and vegetation features. Existing reconstructions of the GLO data for the Coquille River basin such as those by Benner (1991) have primarily focused on the Bandon Reach.

In addition to the GLO mapping, the USGS surveyed channel planforms and profiles for the South Fork Coquille River in 1926 (table 5). LiDAR topographic data collected in 2008 provide a 1-m resolution topographic survey of the entire study area except for the upper 2 km of the study area on the South Fork Coquille River (table 5). Major geologic units and geomorphic divisions of the river basin are depicted in the digital compilation of Oregon geologic maps (Ma and others, 2009). English and Coe (2011) mapped channel migration and potential hazard areas along the South Fork Coquille River and mainstem from approximately RKM 113.4–103.2 near Powers and approximately RKM 76.8–2.4 from the towns of Broadbent to Bandon.

Table 4. Available aerial photographs by reach for the Coquille River study area, southwestern Oregon. Aerial photographs shown in bold were used to delineate bar and channel features for this study

[RKM, river kilometer; ~, approximately; USACE, U.S. Army Corps of Engineers; UO, University of Oregon Map and Aerial Photography Library; --, not applicable; NA, not available; USGS, U.S. Geological Survey; USDA, U.S. Department of Agriculture; WAC, Western Aerial Contractor; OSDR, Oregon State Department of Revenue; AM; Aerial Mapping; BLM, Bureau of Land Management; m, meter]

Full coverage of reach(es)	Partial coverage of reach(es)	Year	Collection month/day	Scale	Collection entity	Repository
All reaches except Powers	**Powers (RKM 108–96.9)**	**1939**	**Multiple dates[1]**	**~1:10,200**	**USACE**	**USACE, UO**
All reaches	--	1942	NA	1:27,200	USGS	UO
All reaches	--	1954	NA	1:20,000	USDA	UO
Myrtle Point, Bandon, Gravelford	Broadbent (RKM 70–66.2)	1956	11/24	1:10,000	WAC	USACE
Bandon	Myrtle Point (RKM 60.4–58.5)	1956	11/23	1:24,000	WAC	USACE
Powers, Broadbent, Myrtle Point, Gravelford	Bandon (RKM 58.5–52, 40–7.2)	1957	2/12; 2/17	1:9,600	USACE	USACE
Bridge	Bandon (RKM 40–16.2)	1957	4/26	1:10,000	USACE	USACE
--	Bandon (RKM 7.2–0)	1964	4/13	1:24,000	USACE	USACE
All reaches	--	**1967**	**5/8; 5/25**	**1:20,000**	**USDA**	**UO**
--	Bandon (RKM 58–11.4), Gravelford (~RKM 3–0)	1972	6/4	1:12,000	WAC	USACE
--	Bandon (RKM 11.4–0)	1972	5/18	1:12,000	WAC	USACE
All reaches	--	1976	NA	1:12,000	OSDR	UO
--	Bandon (RKM 56.2–0)	1978	5/19	1:12,000	AM	USACE
Bandon	--	1978	9/23	1:24,000	AM	USACE
Bandon	Myrtle Point (RKM 60.4–58.5)	1978	10/18	1:24,000	AM	USACE
--	Bandon (RKM 56.2–0)	1980	6/29–30	1:12,000	AM	USACE
--	Bandon (intermittent coverage RKM 56.3–40, all RKM 10–0)	1982	3/23	1:48,000	WAC	USACE
All reaches	--	1982	NA	1:80,000	USGS	UO
--	Bandon (RKM 10–0)	1983	9/16	1:48,000	WAC	USACE
Powers, Broadbent, Myrtle Point, Bandon	Gravelford (RKM 10–0), Bridge (RKM 7.1–0)	1986	6/12	1:48,000	WAC	USACE
All reaches	--	1986	NA	1:12,000	BLM	UO
Broadbent, Myrtle Point, Bandon	Powers (RKM 114.8–96.9)	1989	11/2	1:24,000	Bergman	USACE
--	Gravelford (intermittent coverage)	1990	7/20	1:24,000	Bergman	USACE
All reaches	--	1995	Multiple dates[2]	1 pixel = 1 m	USGS	USGS; UO

Table 4. Available aerial photographs by reach for the Coquille River study area, southwestern Oregon. Aerial photographs shown in bold were used to delineate bar and channel features for this study—continued

[RKM, river kilometer; ~, approximately; USACE, U.S. Army Corps of Engineers; UO, University of Oregon Map and Aerial Photography Library; --, not applicable; NA, not available; USGS, U.S. Geological Survey; USDA, U.S. Department of Agriculture; WAC, Western Aerial Contractor; OSDR, Oregon State Department of Revenue; AM; Aerial Mapping; BLM, Bureau of Land Management; m, meter]

Full coverage of reach(es)	Partial coverage of reach(es)	Year	Collection month/day	Scale	Collection entity	Repository
All reaches	--	2000–01	Multiple dates[3]	1 pixel = 1 m	USGS	USGS
--	Bandon (intermittent coverage RKM 52–19, all RKM 19–0)	2001	5/10	1:24,000	WAC	USACE
Myrtle Point	Broadbent (RKM 75.2–66.2), Bandon (RKM 58.5–52)	2001	5/18	1:24,000	WAC	USACE
All reaches	**--**	**2005**	**07/15; 08/5**	**1 pixel = 0.5 m**	**USDA**	**USGS**
All reaches	**--**	**2009**	**Multiple dates[4]**	**1 pixel = 1 m**	**USDA**	**USGS**
All reaches	--	2011	Multiple dates[5]	1 pixel = 1 m	USDA	USGS

[1] 5/3, 5/5, 7/17

[2] 5/1–3, 5/6/, 5/27, 5/30, 8/5

[3] 7/27/2000, 8/08/2000, 8/12/2000, 8/17/2000, 8/21/2000, 7/14/2001, 7/23/2001

[4] 6/17-18, 6/22, 7/15

[5] 6/17, 6/20, 7/5

Table 5. Datasets reviewed for this study in the Coquille River basin, southwestern Oregon

[BLM, Bureau of Land Management; RKM, river kilometer; NA, not available; USCS, U.S. Coast Survey; NOAA, National Oceanic and Atmospheric Administration; USGS, U.S. Geological Survey; OSU, Oregon State University; ODFW, Oregon Department of Fish and Wildlife; DOGAMI, Oregon Department of Geology and Mineral Industries; LiDAR, Light Detection and Ranging; m, meter]

Dataset	Scale	Date(s)	Source	Depository	Description
General Land Office Surveys (GLO)	~1:31,680	1857–76	GLO maps	BLM[1]	Earliest surveys conducted in 1857–59; meander surveys conducted in 1857, 1867, 1871, and 1874; study areas on the mainstem and North Fork Coquille River are meandered; South Fork Coquille River is meandered to RKM 108.7; maps show planview of river and surrounding lands; limited details on channel features; See Brenner (1991) for additional GLO information
Reconnaissance of Entrance & Part of Coquille River	NA	1861	USCS	NOAA[2]	Bathymetric map of ~RKM 4.8–0 of Coquille River
Bathymetric survey	NA	1905	USACE; Farnell (1979)	USACE	Bathymetric map of ~RKM 0.8–0 of the Coquille River following jetty improvements
Plan and profile of Coquille River (South Fork), Oregon	1:31,680	1926	USGS	OSU; USGS	Contour map of Coquille River in study area from RKM 105 to 115.4 on the South Fork Coquille River; includes profiles
Nautical chart of the Coquille River entrance	1:10,000	Multiple dates[3]	USCS	NOAA[2]	Bathymetric map of ~RKM 6.2–0 of Coquille River
Habitat map of the Coquille estuary	NA	1978	ODFW	OSU[4]	Map of estuary categorized by tidal inundation, habitat type, vegetation, and sediment for RKM 8–0
LiDAR	~1 m	2008	DOGAMI	DOGAMI	High resolution topographic survey of basin, complete coverage of study area except for RKM 113.4–115.4 on South Fork Coquille River
Geologic map	1:12,000– 1:500,000	2009	DOGAMI	DOGAMI	Digital compilation of geologic maps in Oregon (Ma and others, 2009); full coverage
Channel migration hazard maps	1:6,000– 1:12,000	2011	DOGAMI;	DOGAMI	Maps identifying potential channel migration zones derived from LiDAR and repeat aerial photography from ~RKM 113.4–103.2, 76.8–2.4 (English and Coe, 2011)
Bathymetric survey	1:1,000	2011	USACE	USACE[5]	Bathymetric map of ~RKM 2–0 of Coquille River

[1] BLM website: *http://www.blm.gov/or/landrecords/survey/ySrvy1.php*

[2] NOAA website: *http://historicalcharts.noaa.gov/*

[3] 1945, 1967, 1971, 1973, 1977, 1978, 1981, 1987, 1992, 2000, 2003, 2004

[4] OSU library: *http://oregondigital.org/digcol/index.php*

[5] USACE website: *http://www.nwp.usace.army.mil/navigation/*

The Bandon Reach has several additional topographic and bathymetric datasets that could support assessments of channel condition and change for the lower Coquille River. For example, the U.S. Coast Survey surveyed the lower Coquille River in 1861 (table 5). Several recent bathymetric surveys of approximately the lower 6 km of the Coquille River were performed by the U.S. Coast Survey, whereas a 2011 survey by the Corps of Engineers collected bathymetry for approximately the lower 2 km of the Coquille River (table 5).

Previous Hydrologic and Geomorphic Studies

A search for previous hydrologic and geomorphic studies in the Coquille River basin yielded few studies that directly addressed hydrology, channel geomorphology, and sediment dynamics. Here, we summarize two geomorphic studies on the South Fork Coquille River by Florsheim and Williams (1996) and Clearwater Biostudies, Inc. (2003) and a channel migration hazards study on the South Fork and mainstem Coquille River by English and Coe (2011). A summary of more general watershed analyses describing bed-material and channel condition for several tributaries joining the South Fork Coquille River above the study area is provided by Peck and Park (2006).

Florsheim and Williams (1996) summarized watershed geomorphic and hydrologic processes contributing to bank erosion in a short section (RKM 75.1–66.2) of the Broadbent Reach on the South Fork Coquille River. Within this section, banks were composed of unconsolidated silty clay loam and silt loam, and were described as eroded to vertical profiles and with heights exceeding 7.6 m in several locations (Florsheim and Williams, 1996). Using aerial photographs, they estimated that approximately 40,469 m^2 of riparian land had been lost from 1939 to 1992 owing to bank erosion at channel bends or erosion of areas lacking riparian vegetation (Florsheim and Williams, 1996). On the basis of their observations, including the presence of tall (7.6 m) and steep banks and the elevation differences between the channel bed and floodplain, Florsheim and Williams (1996) concluded that the channel in this section is likely incising and adjusting to a reduction in sediment supply (after a substantial loading of sediment during the late 1800s) as a result of instream gravel mining and recently implemented forestry practices that reduce hill-slope erosion.

Clearwater Biostudies, Inc. (2003) conducted a riparian and geomorphic assessment of the South Fork Coquille River from the Siskiyou National Forest Boundary (approximately 350 m upstream of the Powers Reach) to its confluence with the North Fork Coquille River (RKM 58.5), encompassing the Powers, Broadbent, and Myrtle Point Reaches. They determined that eroding banks generally lacked woody riparian vegetation, increased in number and/or severity from RKM 64.2 to 59.8, and reached heights of 7.6–9.1 m in several locations (Clearwater Biostudies, Inc., 2003). They attributed bank instability to the lack of riparian vegetation and changes in channel planform following the installation of rock structures for bank protection (Clearwater Biostudies, Inc., 2003). The authors reported that the South Fork Coquille River had a moderate sediment supply and a channel with either stable or unknown condition above Dement Creek (RKM 82.4), but moderate to high sediment inputs and indicators of channel aggradation and incision below Dement Creek (Clearwater Biostudies, 2003). In particular, they noted that channel instability was greatest from RKM 78.4 to 76.9 owing to bank erosion and increases in channel width and sinuosity after the November 1996 flood (Clearwater Biostudies, 2003). Although they did not detect any differences in gravel surface area up- and downstream of Dement Creek, they noted that exposed bar area was lowest from RKM 64.2 to 63 near sites of instream gravel mining and that gravel deposits were more extensive along the lower South Fork Coquille River in 1939 than in 1997 (Clearwater Biostudies, Inc., 2003). Particle measurements indicated that median particle sizes (D_{50}) ranged from 1 to 243 millimeters (mm) in riffles within the river, and fine sediments (derived possibly from natural deposition, tributary sources, and bank erosion) increased in riffles as the river approached its confluence the North Fork Coquille River, particularly from approximately RKM 61.8 to 59.8 (Clearwater Biostudies, Inc., 2003).

Clearwater Biostudies, Inc. (2003) also assessed patterns in channel planform using field data collected in 2001 and historical spatial data. On the basis of their field measurements of channel width at 206 locations, they determined that channel widths varied by a factor of 7 within their study area, indicating frequent adjustments in channel width and the potential for the channel to locally widen or narrow. Comparison of river position from maps dating from approximately 1870 and 1980 suggests that channel alignment and sinuosity changed little between Powers and Dement Creek (RKM 68.9–63.0) and the confluences of the South Fork with the Middle and North Forks of the Coquille River (approximately RKM 60.8–59.8). This analysis, however, did indicate a 14-percent reduction in channel sinuosity, a 12-percent reduction in channel length, and loss in river bend frequency between Broadbent and the Middle Fork Coquille River (approximately RKM 61.8–61.4) as well as a 5-percent reduction in both sinuosity and channel length between Dement Creek and Broadbent (RKM 62.2–61.8) (Clearwater Biostudies, Inc., 2003). The authors also concluded that (1) decreases in channel length reflect channel incision and increasing channel slope and bank heights, (2) further comparison of their results and those of Florsheim and Williams (1996) suggest that historical changes in channel meander patterns generally occurred prior to 1939, and (3) channel width did not increase systematically in a downstream direction, but varied throughout the study section (Clearwater Biostudies, Inc., 2003). They also state that the river channel was clearly incised in the 1939 photographs, but do not document the basis of this statement (Clearwater Biostudies, Inc., 2003).

In a channel-migration hazard study, English and Coe (2011) reviewed aerial and orthophotographs taken from 1939 to 2005 and the LiDAR topographic data collected in 2008 (table 5) to identify locations along the South Fork and mainstem Coquille River where lateral channel migration may be expected in the future. English and Coe (2011) reported that most channel migration along the South Fork Coquille River occurred between Broadbent and Myrtle Point (approximately RKM 75.2–60.4) and between two time periods (1942–1967, 1968–1996), coinciding with the large floods of 1964 and 1996 (fig. 4B). They also identified several avulsion-prone areas (such as RKM 75.1–71.2, 70.4–68.8, and 67–66; fig. 9) in the Broadbent Reach, a large historically active avulsion area south of the town of Coquille (near RKM 51.2; fig. 11), and two paleo-channels southwest of Coquille (starting near RKM 45; fig. 11; English and Coe, 2011). Near Powers, they noted bank erosion (in some locations up to 13 m in a 50-year period) and mass wasting that can lead to channel widening and increased sediment fluxes to downstream sections (English and Coe, 2011).

Gravel-Operator Information and Surveys

In June 2011, we reviewed permit files at the Oregon Department of State Lands (DSL) to obtain estimates of deposited and mined volumes of bed material reported for instream gravel mining sites in the Coquille River basin. Although some permit files included notes describing mining activities in the 1930s, mined volume estimates were mainly available from 1974 to 78 for 12 operators in the Coquille River basin and from 1996 to 2009 for 9 sites on the South Fork Coquille River. Estimates from the 1970s appeared to be based primarily on operator estimates, whereas more recent estimates were based predominantly on repeat topographic surveys at the mining sites.

From 1974 to 1978, a total gravel volume of at least 306,600 m^3 was mined from multiple sites on Salmon Creek, the South and Middle Forks of the Coquille River, and mainstem (table 6). For this period, total reported annual mined volumes ranged from at least 58,700 to 68,300 m^3. Reported annual mined volumes were greatest for the multiple sites operated by Benham Concrete Co. on the South Fork Coquille River (22,900 m^3 reported per year) and by the Oregon State Highway Division on the Middle Fork Coquille River (15,300 m^3 reported per year). Although changes in channel position and site ownership made it challenging to assess and track mining operations at each location over time, gravel mining likely has occurred more recently at sites such as the Lokan, Herman, Broadbent, Coos Highway, Thompson, and Hayes Bars in the Broadbent Reach of the South Fork Coquille River (fig. 9).

Table 6. Compilation of reported gravel volumes mined from 1974 to 1978 in the Coquille River basin, southwestern Oregon.

[m^3, cubic meter; RKM, river kilometer; --, data gaps; data compiled from permit files housed at Oregon Department of State Lands (accessed 6/2011)]

River/Creek	Operator	Reported mined volumes (m³)					Ongoing mining site (if available)
		1974	1975	1976	1977	1978	
Salmon Creek	Merchen and Reed Gravel Company	5,000	5,000	2,700	2,400	600	--
South Fork Coquille River	Benham Concrete Company	22,900	22,900	22,900	22,900	22,900	Lokan, Herman, and Broadbent Bars
	Oregon State Highway Division	3,800	--	3,100	--	3,800	--
	Coos County Highway Department	7,900	7,900	7,900	7,900	7,900	Coos Highway Bar
	Oregon State Highway Division	--	5,700	--	--	5,700	--
	Train Farms	1,900	1,900	1,900	1,900	--	--
	Merchen and Reed Gravel Company	6,100	13,700	4,600	9,900	2,500	Thompson Bar
	Clyde D. Lundy	800	800	--	--	--	Hayes Bar
	Gordon Hayes	--	--	1,500	1,500	2,300	Hayes Bar
	Merchen and Reed Gravel Company	--	--	2,100	--	200	--
Middle Fork Coquille River	Oregon State Highway Division	15,300	15,300	15,300	15,300	15,300	--
Coquille River	Coos County Highway Department, Parks	--	100	100	100	100	--
Cumulative annual mined volume		58,700	68,300	59,400	59,500	60,700	

From 1996 to 2009, estimates of deposited and mined gravel volumes were reported for eight and nine sites, respectively, in the Broadbent Reach of the South Fork Coquille River (tables 7 and 8; fig. 14A–I). During this period, the cumulative deposition volumes per site ranged from at least 10,500 to 176,100 m^3, with the mean annual deposition per site exceeding 3,000 m^3 at the Hayes, Elliot, Seals, Broadbent, and Herman Bars (table 7). For all sites, the cumulative surveyed deposition totaled at least 485,600 m^3 during this period, and the annual average deposited volume was 34,700 m^3/yr (table 8).

The reported cumulative mining volumes at each site ranged from 2,000 to 81,600 m^3, and the mean annual mining volumes exceeded 3,000 m^3 at the Hayes and Broadbent Bars (table 7). From 1996 to 2009, the reported cumulative volume of gravel mined from the Broadbent Reach of the South Fork Coquille River was at least 207,100 m^3, or approximately 43 percent of the reported volume of deposited sediment (table 8). On average, nearly 15,000 m^3 per year was reported as mined from the Broadbent Reach from 1996 to 2009 (table 8). Actual mined and deposited volumes may have been greater than indicated by this compilation of available data because volumes were not reported for several sites and years (table 7).

The available estimates of deposited and mined gravel volumes for sites on the South Fork Coquille River indicate that bed material transported by the river mostly rebuilds mined bar surfaces (table 7; fig. 14A–I). Cumulative deposition volumes were greatest following the 2-year recurrence-interval flood on December 2, 1998 (WY 1999; table 8; fig. 4B) and 50-year recurrence-interval flood on November 18, 1996 (WY 1997; table 8; fig. 4B). For individual sites with multiple deposition estimates, however, annual deposition volumes varied between sites and years. Deposition at the Hayes and Elliot Bars was slightly greater in 1997 than in 1999, whereas deposition was greatest at Seals Bar (located at RKM 88.8 opposite of Elliot Bar) in 2004 (table 7; fig. 14C). Differences in deposition patterns between the adjacent Seals and Elliot Bars are likely related to local channel hydraulics and changes in deposition patterns evident in the repeat bar mapping described below. Meanwhile, deposition was greatest in 1999 at the Broadbent and Herman Bars (table 7; fig. 14E, G) and in 2000 at Isenhart Bar (table 7; fig. 14F). Compared with other sites, estimated deposition volumes have been markedly lower since 2005 at Broadbent Bar and since 2001 at Lokan Bar (table 7).

Because gravel mining likely creates preferential depositional areas on mined bar surfaces, these deposition estimates at individual bars cannot be reliably extrapolated to assess overall deposition rates for all bars along the South Fork Coquille River. However, these estimates do indicate that annual deposition volumes at mined bars averaged over 34,700 m^3 from 1996 to 2009 (table 8), suggesting that the annual bed-material transport in the South Fork Coquille River at least exceeded this value.

Our repeat delineation of bar and channel features shows that several of these mined bars changed in size, shape, or position relative to the main channel from 1939 to 2009 (see "Delineation of Bar and Channel Features, 1939–2009" section). Detailed analyses of bed-material flux and morphological changes along the South Fork Coquille River would enable more quantitative assessments of changes in bar replenishment and morphology in relation to peak flows as well as support the evaluation of possible effects of gravel mining on overall bed-material flux and downstream channel conditions. Historical aerial photographs such as those taken in 1995 and 2000 (table 4) would likely support such a detailed geomorphic assessment.

Table 7. Compilation of reported gravel volumes deposited and mined from 1996 to 2009 at instream mining sites in the Broadbent Reach of the South Fork Coquille River, southwestern Oregon

[Hwy, highway; m³, cubic meter; RKM, river kilometer; --, data gaps; data compiled from permit files housed at Oregon Department of State Lands (accessed 6/2011)]

	Bar name and location (RKM)							
	Hayes 93.8, 93.3, 92.3		Elliot 88.8		Seals 88.8		Thompson 87.9, 87.4, 87.1	
	Volume deposited (+) or mined (–)(m³)							
Year	+	–	+	–	+	–	+	–
1996	11,200	--	2,300	--	4,000	--	0	0
1997	26,100	--	10,400	--	3,600	--	6,500	7,000
1998	15,600	6,100	6,000	3,400	4,300	0	6,500	5,000
1999	25,500	19,300	10,200	5,600	4,900	5,300	--	0
2000	13,200	8,800	2,100	3,200	2,900	2,800	--	0
2001	6,100	--	3,100	--	3,400	--	--	0
2002	7,500	11,900	--	1,100	--	3,600	--	0
2003	9,800	5,000	3,400	1,800	4,700	2,100	--	0
2004	7,700	0	1,700	0	9,200	0	--	0
2005	12,600	9,800	--	--	4,800	5,800	--	0
2006	15,500	13,300	4,600	2,200	5,200	4,600	--	0
2007	--	--	--	--	--	--	--	0
2008	9,200	--	1,800	--	5,200	--	--	0
2009	16,100	7,400	5,000	2,000	8,100	1,800	--	0
Mean annual volume by site	13,500	9,100	4,600	2,400	5,000	2,900	1,100	900
Cumulative volume by site	176,100	81,600	50,600	19,300	60,300	26,000	13,000	12,000

Table 7. Compilation of reported gravel volumes deposited and mined from 1996 to 2009 at instream mining sites in the Broadbent Reach of the South Fork Coquille River, southwestern Oregon—continued.

[Hwy, highway; m³, cubic meter; RKM, river kilometer; --, data gaps; data compiled from permit files housed at Oregon Department of State Lands (accessed 6/2011)]

	Bar name and location (RKM)									
	Broadbent 83		Isenhart 81.8		Herman 79		Lokan 76.4		Coos County Hwy 80.2, 75.9	
	Volume deposited (+) or mined (–)(m³)									
Year	+	–	+	–	+	–	+	–	+	–
1996	11,200	--	--	--	--	--	--	--	--	--
1997	15,200	--	3,100	--	2,900	--	--	--	--	--
1998	11,800	--	3,200	0	3,600	0	5,200	3,100	--	--
1999	20,500	19,800	2,900	1,900	5,000	3,200	--	--	--	--
2000	12,300	0	4,100	1,800	3,500	3,000	1,200	1,000	--	--
2001	--	--	500	--	--	700	600	--	--	0
2002	19,600	8,700	900	0	1,500	1,500	300	0	--	2,000
2003	7,100	11,200	2,800	600	4,100	1,400	500	0	--	0
2004	12,000	0	2,300	0	3,400	0	800	0	--	--
2005	1,400	1,900	--	0	2,200	2,000	500	0	--	0
2006	2,000	2,200	--	--	--	--	800	--	--	0
2007	--	--	--	--	--	--	--	--	--	--
2008	1,200	--	3,600	--	4,700	--	600	--	--	--
2009	2,200	500	--	--	4,300	1,700	--	--	--	--
Mean annual volume by site	9,700	5,538	2,600	600	3,500	1,500	1,200	300	--	200
Cumulative volume by site	116,500	44,300	23,400	4,300	35,200	13,500	10,500	4,100	--	2,000

South Fork Coquille River, upstream of RKM 79

Table 8. Annual summary of reported volumes of deposited and mined gravel from 1996 to 2009 for instream mining sites in the Broadbent Reach of the South Fork Coquille River, southwestern Oregon.

[m^3, cubic meter; --, data gaps; Hwy, highway; data compiled from permit files housed at Oregon Department of State Lands (accessed 6/2011)]

Year	Reported cumulative volumes (m^3)		
	Deposited	Mined	Notes
1996	28,700	--	Only mining inactivity at Thompson Bar reported
1997	67,800	7,000	
1998	56,200	17,600	
1999	69,000	55,100	
2000	39,300	20,600	
2001	13,700	700	
2002	29,800	28,800	
2003	32,400	22,100	
2004	37,100	0	Mining inactivity reported for all sites except for Coos County Hwy Bar
2005	21,500	19,500	
2006	28,100	22,300	
2007	--	--	Only mining inactivity at Thompson Bar reported
2008	26,300	--	Only mining inactivity at Thompson Bar reported
2009	35,700	13,400	
Mean volume	34,700	14,800	
Cumulative volume	485,600	207,100	

South Fork Coquille River, downstream of RKM 79

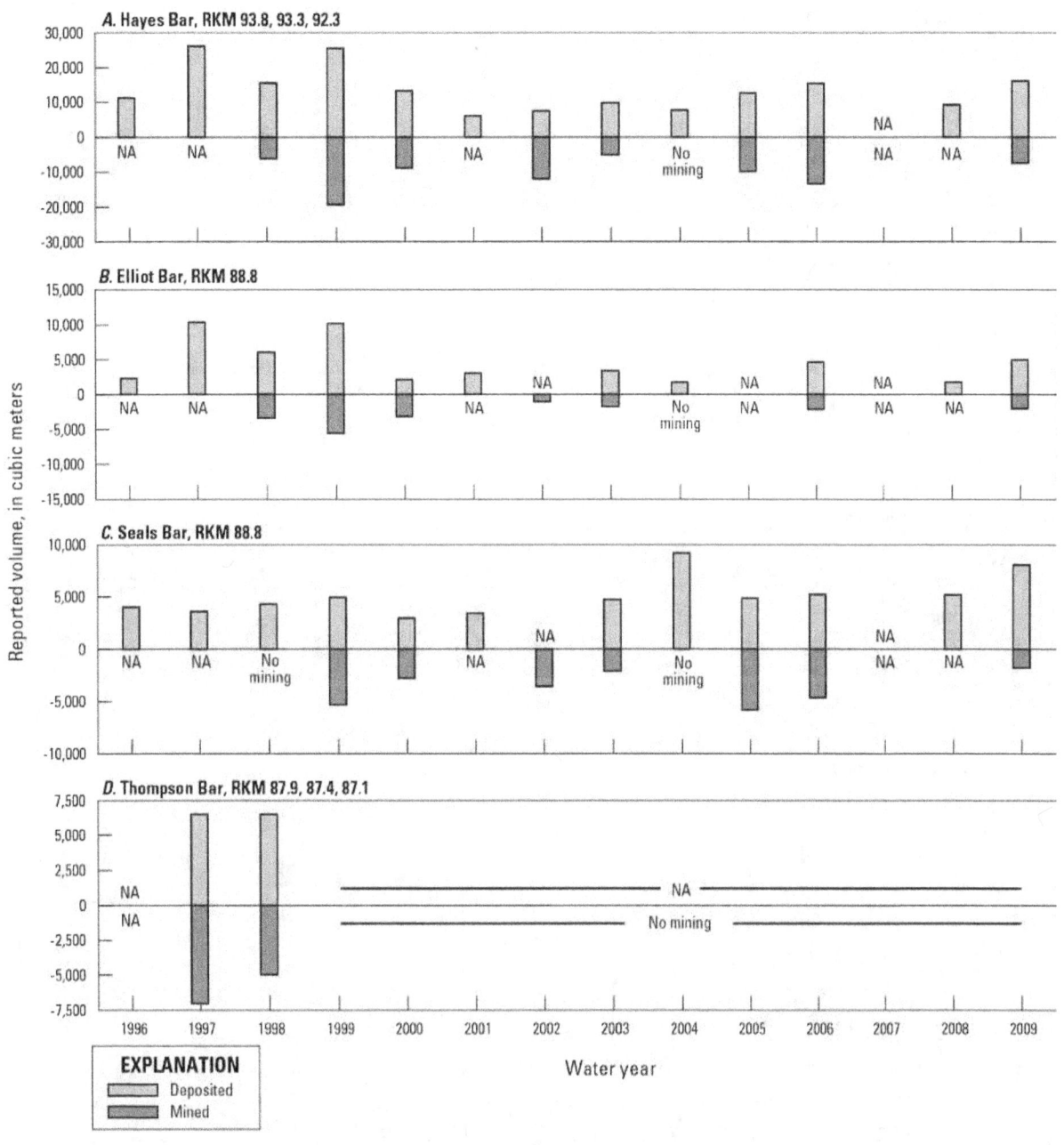

Figure 14. Graphs showing reported estimates of deposited and mined gravel (in cubic meters) from 1996 to 2009 for instream mining sites along the South Fork Coquille River, southwestern Oregon. Data compiled from permit files housed at Oregon Department of State Lands (accessed June 2011).

41

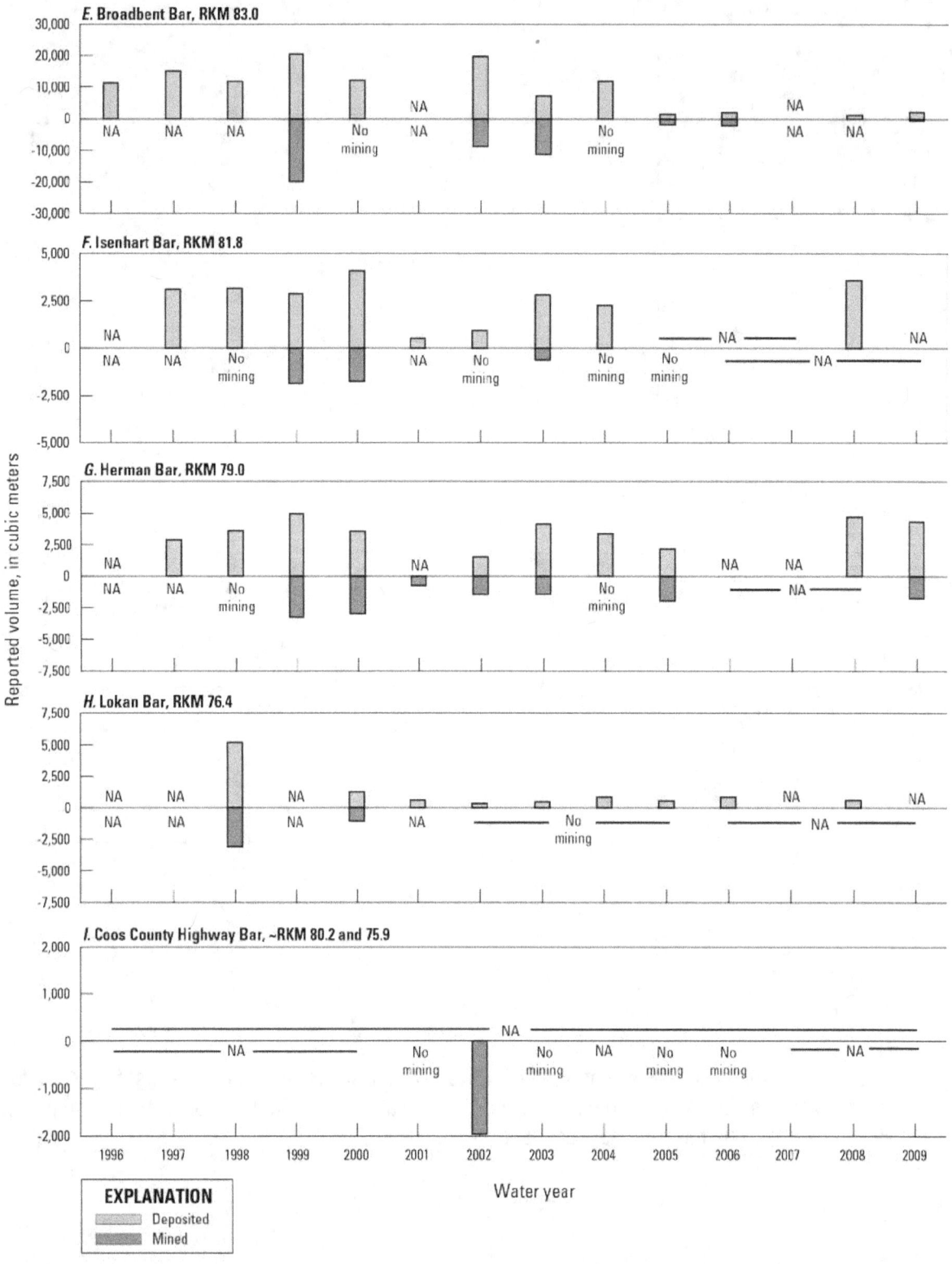

Figure 14 (continued). Graphs showing reported estimates of deposited and mined gravel (in cubic meters) from 1996 to 2009 for instream mining sites along the South Fork Coquille River, southwestern Oregon. Data compiled from permit files housed at Oregon Department of State Lands (accessed June 2011).

Bridge-Inspection Reports

The Oregon Department of Transportation (ODOT) conducts routine bridge inspections to assess overall bridge condition, footing stability, and scour. ODOT's bridge inspection database contains reports for 17 of the 18 bridges within the study area (Oregon Department of Transportation, written commun., 2010; table 9). ODOT has resurveyed channel cross sections near 15 of these bridges, including at least one bridge in each study reach. Sites were surveyed in different years (table 9) with the first surveys conducted between 1992 and 2006 and most recent surveys between 2008 and 2010. Some bridges have had as many as four channel surveys. In addition to examining the resurveyed (or repeat) channel cross sections, we examined supplemental data such as underwater reports, photographs, and scour assessments that are helpful for assessing channel condition and bed material adjacent to the bridges.

A review of the most recent bridge inspection reports indicates that the channels of the South Fork Coquille (RKM 106.1, 103.2, 75.1), mainstem Coquille (RKM 38.9, 5.4), Middle Fork Coquille (RKM 13.8, 12.5, 5.2, 4.9, 2.4, 0.5), and North Fork Coquille Rivers (RKM 0.4) show evidence of bank erosion, such as bank slumping or "minor channel damage" (as stated in ODOT reports). Inspections note signs of bank erosion at nine of these locations as well as scour of the channel and bridge infrastructure at two additional locations (Powers Reach, RKM 108.3; Bridge Reach, RKM 10). The report for the bridge at RKM 89.4 in the Broadbent Reach indicates that the west (or left) abutment was built on an earthflow deposit that moves during winter; this deposit may explain the 1.5–5.1 m erosion along the base of the left bank from 1994 to 2008 (see figure 16A below). Although few bridge inspection reports included notes describing bed material, the bed of the Coquille River was described as sand and silt (Bandon Reach, RKM 38.9) and sand (Bandon Reach, RKM 5.4), whereas the bed of the North Fork Coquille River was described as firm clay (Gravelford Reach, RKM 0.4). Multiple observations document variation in the bed material of the Middle Fork Coquille River as it is sand and cobbles (Bridge Reach, RKM 13.8), sand and gravel (Bridge Reach, RKM 12.5), sand (Bridge Reach, RKM 5.2), and boulder and sand (Bridge Reach, RKM 4.9). No bed observations were available for the South Fork Coquille River.

The repeat cross sections indicate that the channels near bridge crossings in the study area are dynamic and many are subject to channel shifting as well as aggradation or incision (table 9). The patterns of channel change, however, differed between the river segments. On the South Fork and mainstem Coquille River (fig. 15A–B to fig. 17A–B), the thalweg of the channel near three bridges incised more than 0.5 m in elevation over the survey periods; exceptions were near bridges at RKM 108.3 in the Powers Reach (fig. 15A), where the channel flows over bedrock, and RKM 60.3 in the Myrtle Point Reach, where the river is affected by tide (fig. 17A). Incision of the thalweg occurred in the Broadbent Reach of the South Fork Coquille River from 1994 to 2008 as the channel shifted toward the left bank near RKM 89.4 and 75.1 (fig. 16A–B; table 9). In conjunction with the lateral shifting in the Broadbent Reach, the channel banks experienced several meters of deposition and erosion.

The repeat surveys on the Middle and North Forks of the Coquille River showed that changes in channel geometry varied between sites. In the Bridge Reach of the Middle Fork Coquille River, the thalweg incised a net 0.8 m at RKM 13.8, primarily from 1992 to 2000, but then aggraded 1.1 m at RKM 12.5 from 1992 to 2004 and 1.2 m at RKM 2.4 from 2000 to 2004 (fig. 18A–B, F; table 9). Near the other bridges in the Bridge Reach, the elevation of the thalweg was relatively stable while the banks experienced some erosion and deposition (fig. 18C–E, G). In the Gravelford Reach of North Fork Coquille River, the thalweg incised 1.6 m from 2006 to 2008 at RKM 6.6, but aggraded a net 0.8 m from 2000 to 2009 at tidally affected RKM 0.4 (fig. 19A–B; table 9).

Table 9. Summary of net changes measured from channel cross sections surveyed by the Oregon Department of Transportation (ODOT) in the Coquille River study area, southwestern Oregon

[RKM, river kilometer; m, meter; Rd, road; Hwy, highway; --, no data available; St, street; CBR, Coos Bay-Roseburg]

River	Reach	Bridge	RKM	ODOT bridge ID	Survey year(s)	Net thalweg elevation change (m)	Maximum net erosion (m)		Maximum net deposition (m)		Notes
							Left bank	Right bank	Left bank	Right bank	
South Fork Coquille River	Powers	Johnson Mountain Rd	108.3	11C761	1994, 2008	-0.2	-0.5	-0.5	+3.3	+0.4	Relatively stable except for deposition on upper left bank; channel flows over bedrock
		County Hwy 219	106.1	01942A	2001, 2005, 2009	-0.6	-1.5	-1.7	+1.0	+0.6	Thalweg shifted from right to left channel from 2001 to 2005; mid-channel feature aggraded from 2001 to 2005 but then eroded from 2005 to 2009
		Powers Hwy	103.2	017745A	2005	--	--	--	--	--	--
		Baker Creek Lane	100.0	--	--	--	--	--	--	--	Bridge and channel conditions not monitored by ODOT
	Broadbent	Gaylord Rd	89.4	16349	1994, 2008	-1.9	-5.1	0	0	+2.7	Mainly erosion on left bank and deposition on right bank; channel shifted toward left bank
		West Side Rd	75.1	05066A	1994, 2008	-0.6	-0.2	0	+0.5	+1.2	Same as channel near RKM 89.4
Mainstem	Myrtle Point	Spruce St	60.3*	18136	2004, 2008	-0.4	-0.3	-0.1	+1.0	+0.2	Decrease in thalweg elevation; variable bank erosion and deposition
	Bandon	Coquille-Bandon Hwy	38.9*	00589D	2000, 2003, 2010	-0.5	-0.9	-1.8	+2.0	+0.5	Same as channel at RKM 60.3
		Hwy 101	5.4*	07020	2000	--	--	--	--	--	--

44

Table 9. Summary of net changes measured from channel cross sections surveyed by the Oregon Department of Transportation (ODOT) in the Coquille River study area, southwestern Oregon—continued

[RKM, river kilometer; m, meter; Rd, road; Hwy, highway; --, no data available; St, street; CBR, Coos Bay-Roseburg]

River	Reach	Bridge	RKM	ODOT bridge ID	Survey year(s)	Net thalweg elevation change (m)	Maximum net erosion (m)		Maximum net deposition (m)		Notes
							Left bank	Right bank	Left bank	Right bank	
Middle Fork Coquille River	Bridge	CBR Hwy	13.8	08935	1992, 2000, 2004, 2009	-0.8	-0.8	-0.4	+0.5	+0.3	Channel erosion and deposition over time
		CBR Hwy	12.5	08936	1992, 2000, 2004, 2009	+1.1	0	-0.8	+1.6	+0.9	--
		McMullen Rd	10.0	11C65I	1994, 2004, 2008	-0.1	-0.4	-0.3	+0.3	+1.4	Deposition on right bank and in channel from 1994 to 2004; main channel eroded from 2004 to 2008
		CBR Hwy	5.2	08876	2000, 2004, 2010	+0.3	0	0	+0.6	+2.9	Channel deposition from 2000 to 2004 and less from 2004 to 2010; erosion between surveys
		CBR Hwy	4.9	08875	2000, 2004, 2010	-0.1	0	-0.2	+0.4	+0.4	--
		CBR Hwy	2.4	08830	1993, 2000, 2004, 2009	+1.2	-8.3	-2.3	+1.0	+1.3	--
		CBR Hwy	0.5	08842	1993, 2000, 2004, 2009	+0.5	-1	-1.9	+0.9	+0.9	--
North Fork Coquille River	Gravelford	Sitkum Lane	6.6	20127	2006, 2008	-1.6	-2	-1.7	0	0	Deposition in channel but stable geometry
		8th St	0.4*	01056A	2000, 2004, 2009	+0.8	-0.2	-1.3	+1.1	+0.2	Deposition on right bank from 2000 to 2004 that erodes by 2009; thalweg relatively stable from 2000 to 2004, but aggraded and shifted right by 2009; tidally affected

*Bridge within tidally influenced river section

45

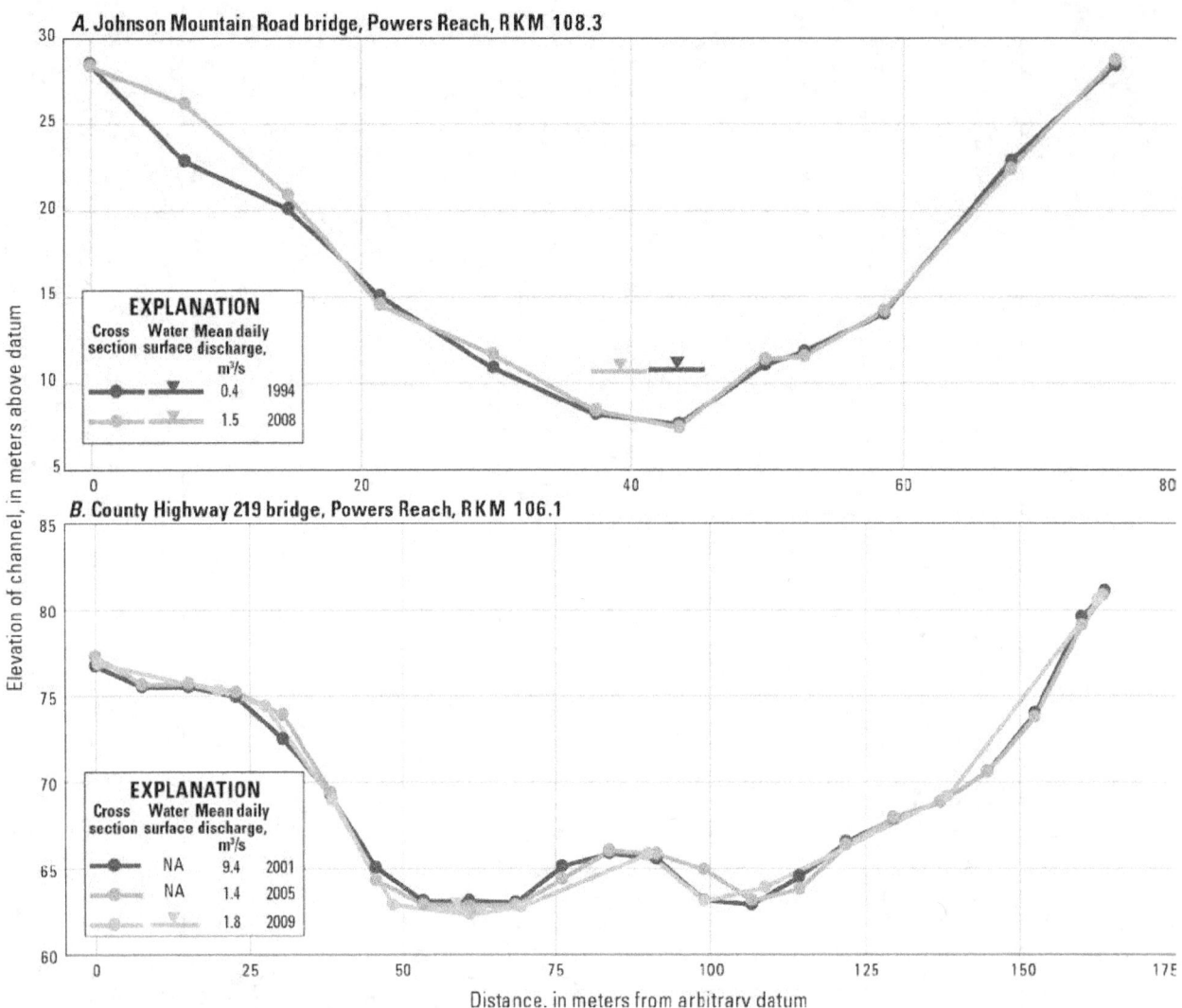

Figure 15. Diagrams showing channel cross sections surveyed at RKM 108.3 and 106.1 in the Powers Reach on the South Fork Coquille River, southwestern Oregon. Data provided by the Oregon Department of Transportation (written commun., 2010). Mean daily discharge record is from the U.S. Geological Survey streamflow-gaging station at Powers, Oregon (14325000) on the South Fork Coquille River for each survey date.

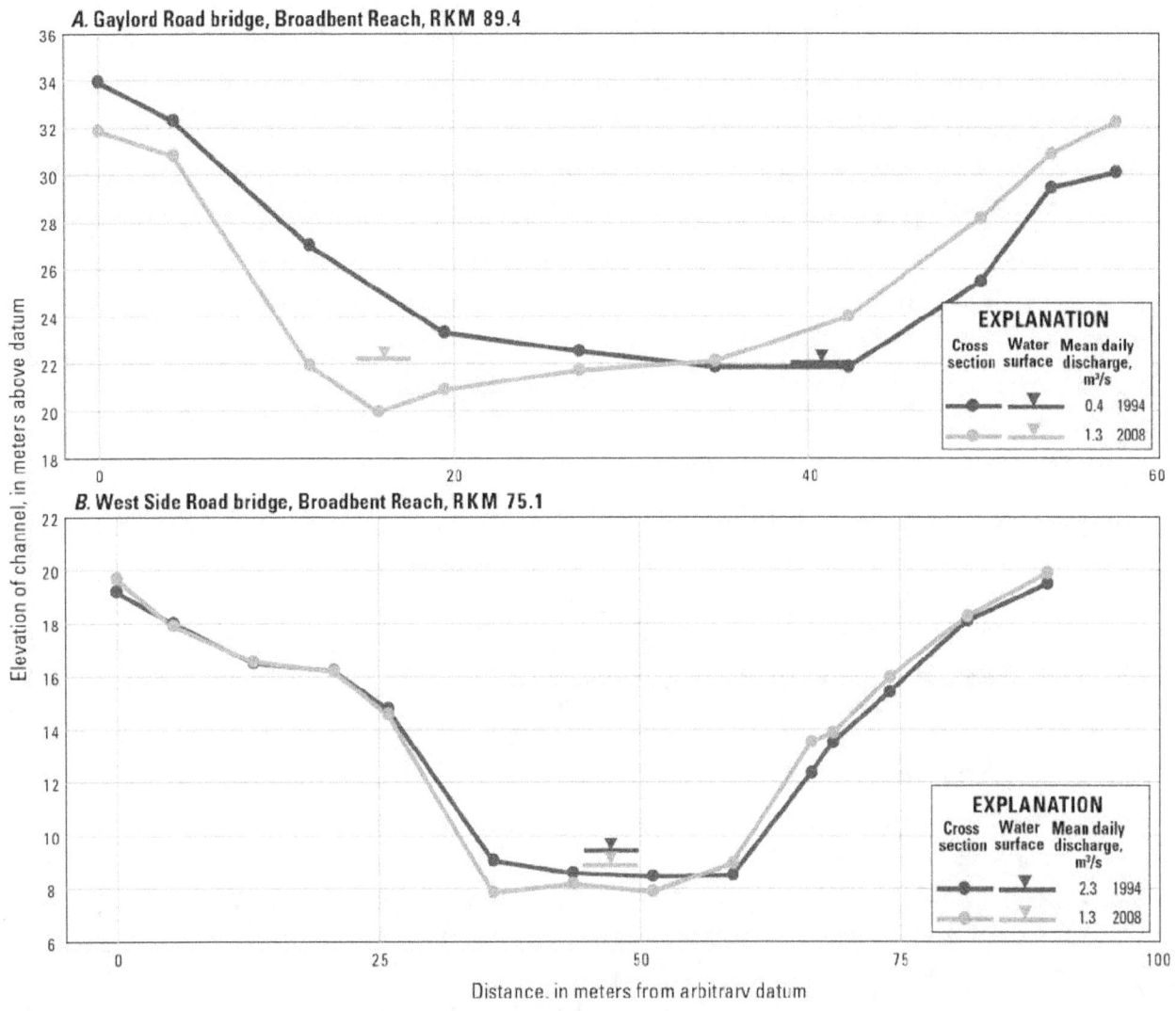

Figure 16. Diagrams showing channel cross sections surveyed at RKM 89.4 and 74.1 in the Broadbent Reach on the South Fork Coquille River, southwestern Oregon. Data provided by the Oregon Department of Transportation (written commun., 2010). Mean daily discharge record is from the U.S. Geological Survey streamflow-gaging station at Powers, Oregon (14325000) on the South Fork Coquille River for each survey date.

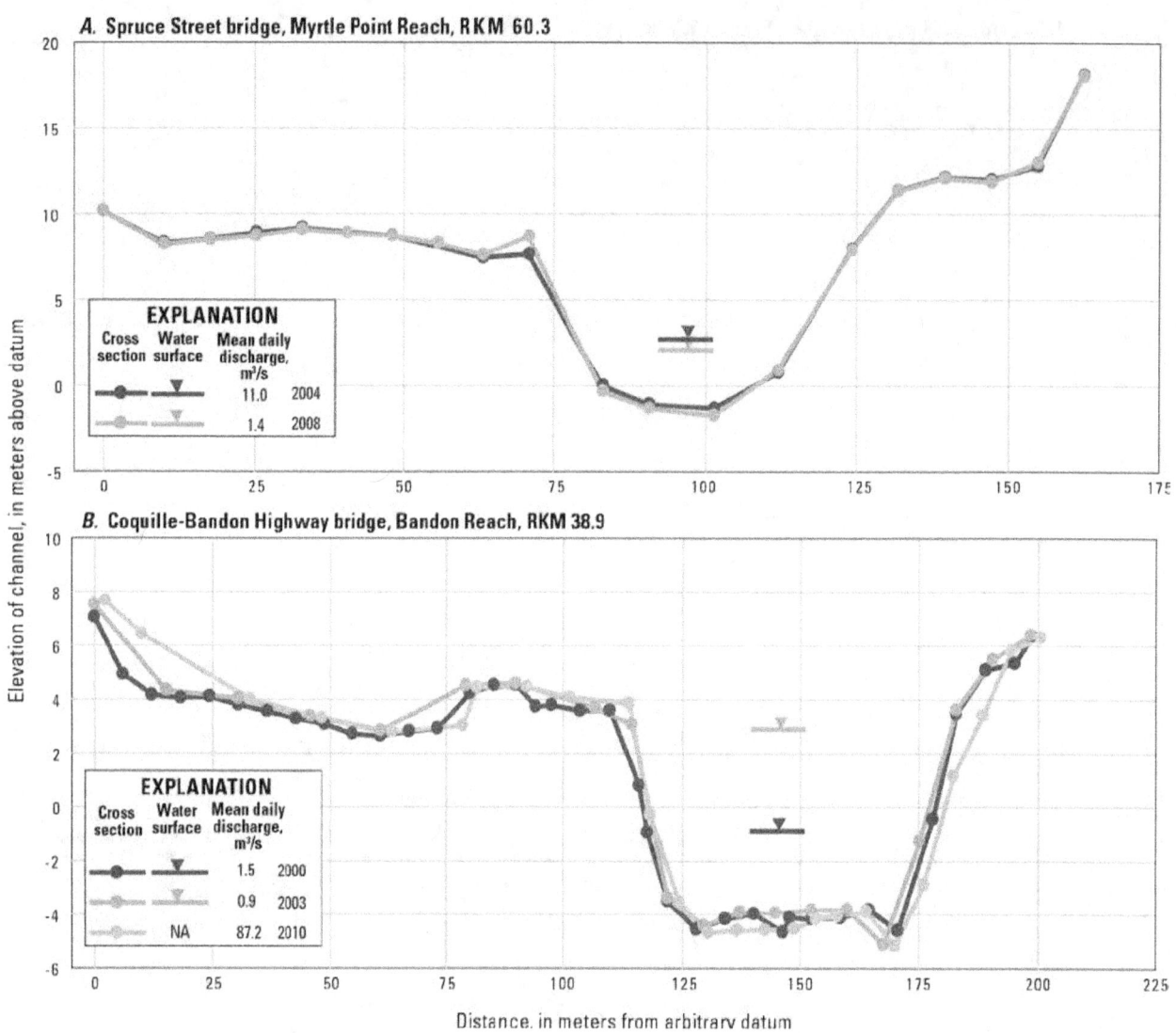

Figure 17. Diagrams showing channel cross sections surveyed at RKM 60.3 in the Myrtle Point Reach of the South Fork Coquille River and RKM 38.9 in the Bandon Reach on the Coquille River, southwestern Oregon. Data provided by the Oregon Department of Transportation (written commun., 2010). Mean daily discharge record is from the U.S. Geological Survey streamflow-gaging station at Powers, Oregon (14325000) on the South Fork Coquille River for each survey date.

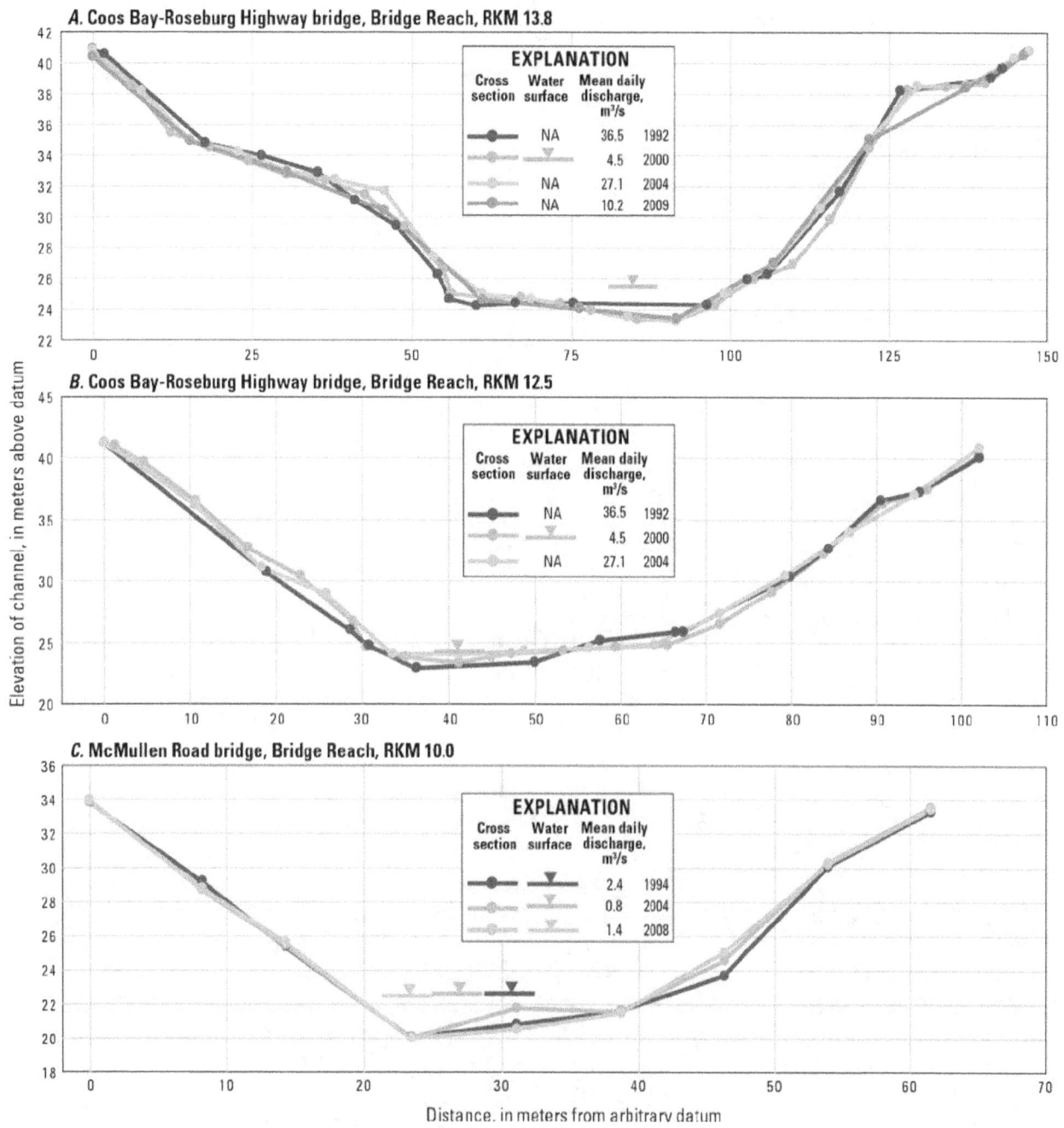

Figure 18. Diagrams showing channel cross sections surveyed at RKM 13.8, 12.5, 10.0, 5.2, 4.9, 2.4, and 0.5 in the Bridge Reach on the Middle Fork Coquille River, southwestern Oregon. Data provided by the Oregon Department of Transportation (written commun., 2010). Mean daily discharge record for each survey date is from the U.S. Geological Survey streamflow-gaging station at Powers, Oregon (14325000) on the South Fork Coquille River because the Middle Fork Coquille River gage near Myrtle Point (14326500) was no longer operational.

49

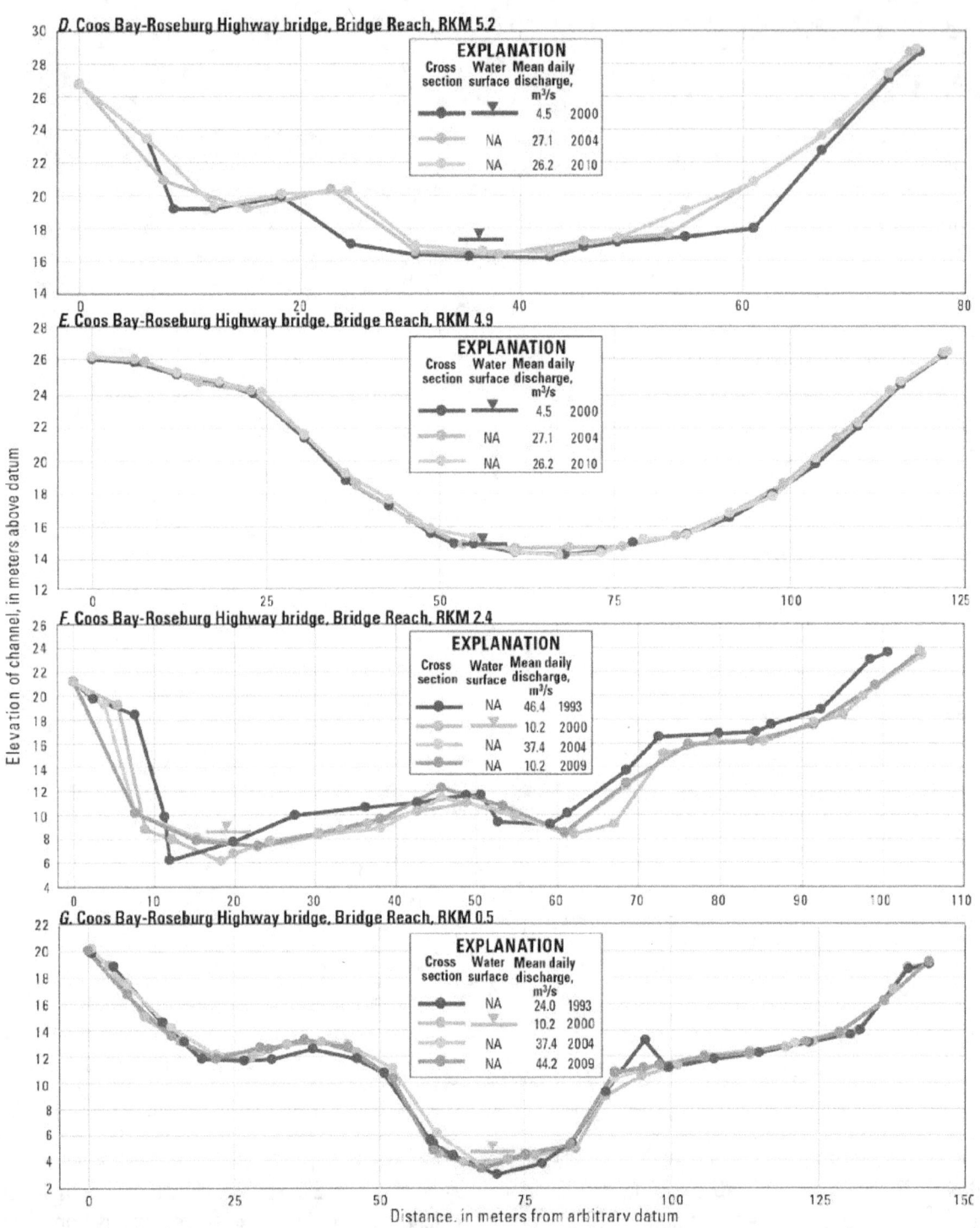

Figure 18 (continued). Diagrams showing channel cross sections surveyed at RKM 13.8, 12.5, 10.0, 5.2, 4.9, 2.4, and 0.5 in the Bridge Reach on the Middle Fork Coquille River, southwestern Oregon. Data provided by the Oregon Department of Transportation (written commun., 2010). Mean daily discharge record for each survey date is from the U.S. Geological Survey streamflow-gaging station at Powers, Oregon (14325000) on the South Fork Coquille River because the Middle Fork Coquille River gage near Myrtle Point (14326500) was no longer operational.

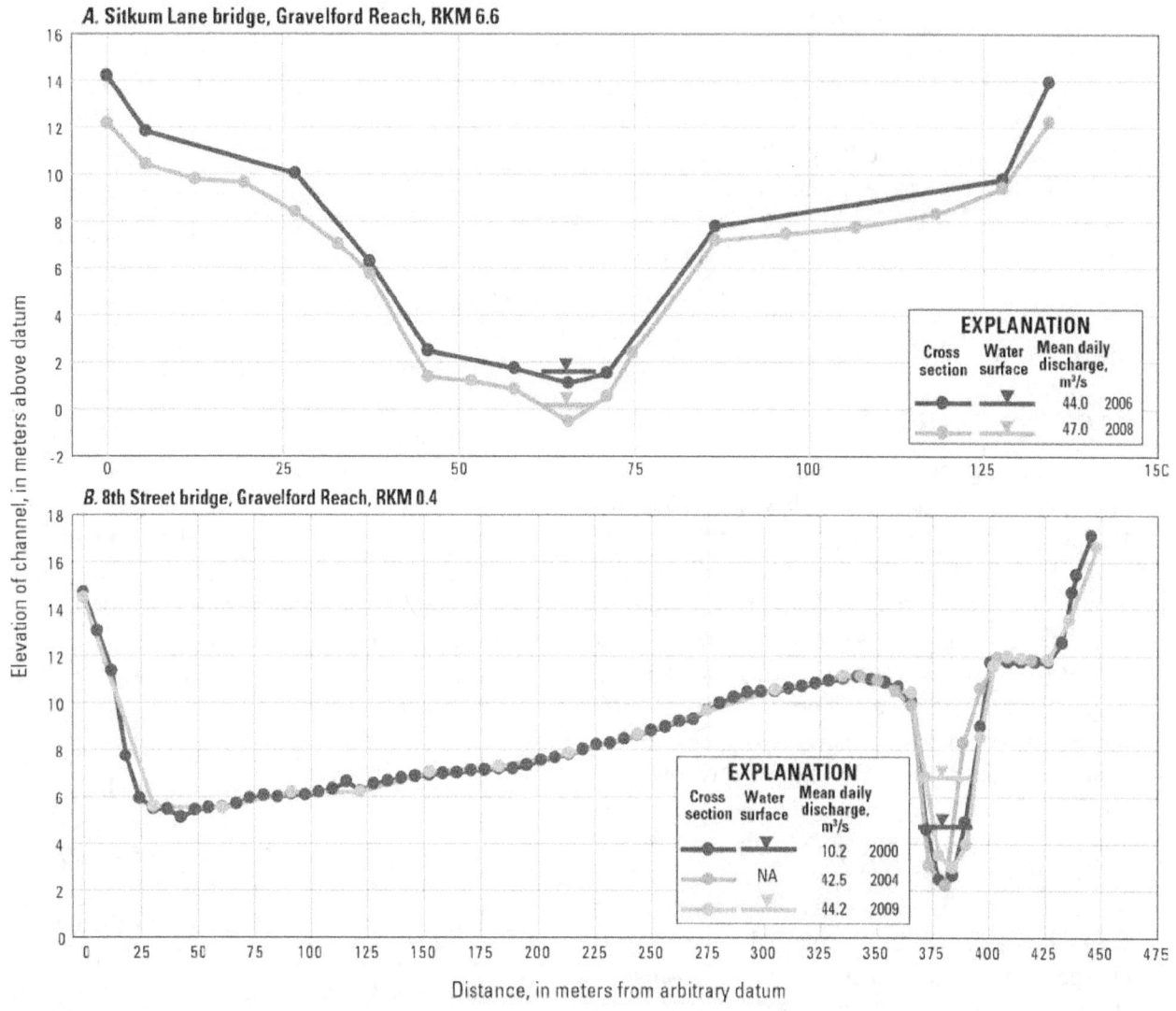

Figure 19. Diagrams showing channel cross sections surveyed at RKM 6.6 and 0.4 in the Gravelford Reach on the North Fork Coquille River, southwestern Oregon. Data provided by the Oregon Department of Transportation (written commun., 2010). Mean daily discharge record for each survey date is from the U.S. Geological Survey streamflow-gaging station at Powers, Oregon (14325000) on the South Fork Coquille River because the North Fork Coquille River gage near Myrtle Point (14327000) was no longer operational.

Near the bridges where the net thalweg elevation changes were less than +/- 0.5 m, substantial cross-section changes include (1) bank aggradation (up to 3.3 m) and erosion (up to 0.5 m) at RKM 108.3 in the Powers Reach from 1994 to 2008 (fig. 15A), (2) aggradation of 1 m near the channel at RKM 60.3 in the Myrtle Point Reach from 2004 to 2008 (fig. 17A), and (3) bank aggradation of 1.4 m from 1994 to 2008 at RKM 10 and 2.9 m from 2000 to 2010 at RKM 5.2 in the Bridge Reach (fig. 18C–D).

Specific Gage Analysis

Following the approach of Klingeman (1973), a specific gage analysis was conducted for the USGS streamflow-gaging station on the South Fork Coquille River at Powers, Oregon (14325000; RKM 105; fig. 1; table 1). Of the available gaging stations (table 1), the gaging station at Powers was selected for this analysis because it has a long-term period of record and is operational as of 2011. The specific gage analysis enables the detection of changes in streambed elevation by assessing changes in water elevation (stage) over time for specific discharge values. At USGS streamflow-gaging stations, discharge is related to stage by a stage-discharge rating curve, which is based on multiple, paired stage and discharge measurements that are taken at a range of streamflows. New rating curves are developed if the channel conditions change substantially (as shown by consistent offsets of newer measurements from the established rating curves) or if a station is relocated. The specific gage analysis evaluates trends in downstream hydraulic control as indicated by the sequence of rating curves; hydraulic control, is in turn a function of bed elevation.

The USGS has collected streamflow records at the Powers gaging station on the South Fork Coquille River (RKM 105) since 1917 (table 1). Because the datum for stage measurements made prior to November 1939 cannot be reliably verified, the analysis period for the specific discharge analysis was November 1939–January 2010. Changes in stage were assessed for low to moderate flows (0.57–87.8 m^3/s) because these flows are more sensitive to minor adjustments in bed elevation and are less likely to be influenced by temporal changes in bank vegetation or bank shape.

From November 1938 to January 2010, the stage-discharge relations for the five analyzed discharges show variations spanning as much as 0.5 m, but all lowered by a net 0.27–0.31 m over the analysis period (fig. 20). Although in-channel bedrock immediately downstream of the gage (such as near RKM 103.6; fig. 8) would serve as a local barrier preventing substantial channel incision from propagating up- or downstream, this general trend of a reduction in stage for specific discharges, indicating either channel incision or widening, is consistent with the channel incision evident in repeat channel cross sections up- and downstream of the gage at RKM 106.1 and 89.4 on the South Fork Coquille River (table 9; figs. 15B and 16A).

Over the period of record, the overall declining stage trend has been interrupted by short periods of rising stage during three periods (1955–1956, 1963–1965, and 1995–1997; fig. 20). These episodes coincide with the floods exceeding a 10-year return period on December 21, 1955, December 22, 1964, and November 18, 1996 (fig. 4B), and perhaps indicate bed-material transport and channel aggradation associated with these relatively large floods. Future review and analysis of station notes, historical cableway surveys, and individual discharge measurements could provide additional information on trends in channel geometry and bed-material at this station.

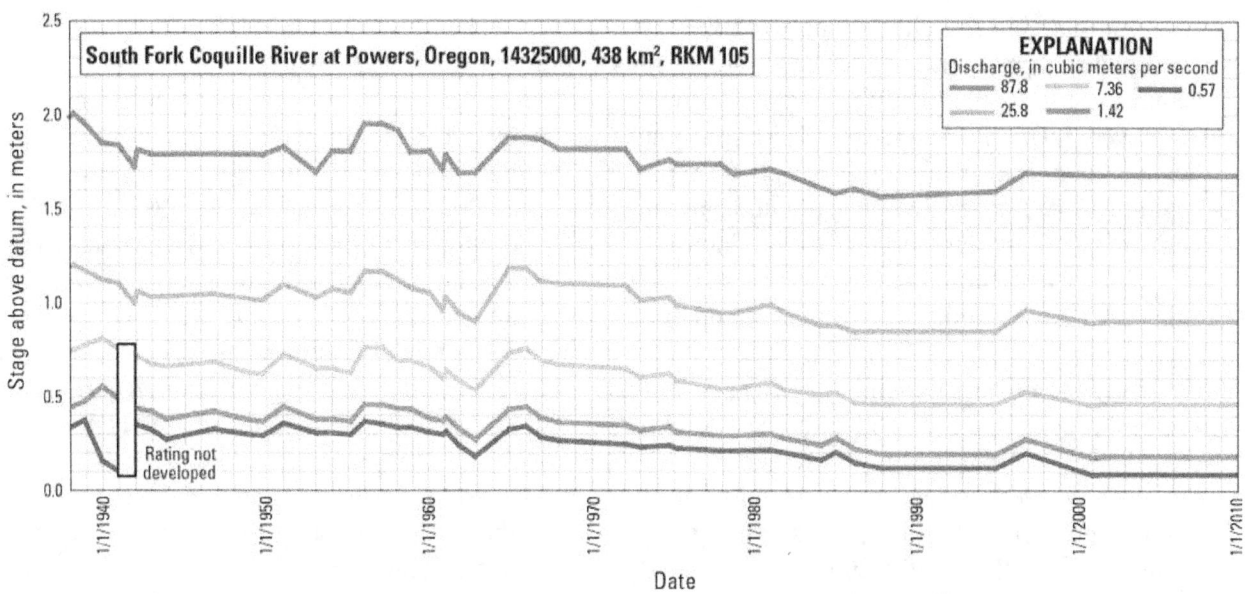

Figure 20. Graph showing the stage-discharge rating curve for specific discharges for the U.S. Geological Survey streamflow-gaging station at Powers (14325000) on the South Fork Coquille River, southwestern Oregon. The source data are station records housed at the Oregon Water Science Center, U.S. Geological Survey, Portland, Oregon.

Delineation of Bars and Channel Features, 1939–2009

For this reconnaissance-level study, we mapped:

1. Channel centerlines for the full study area extent using orthophotographs taken in 2009 (table 4) to develop the linear reference system for this study, and

2. Bars, channel centerlines, and wetted channel edges for the Powers Reach from RKM 108.1 to 96.9 and the full extent of all other reaches using aerial and orthophotographs taken in 1939, 1967, 2005, and 2009 (table 4) to assess temporal changes in the location and areal coverage of bars and the length and wetted width of the channel.

For both efforts, we delineated lateral and medial bars greater than 300 m^2 from aerial and ortho-photographs at a scale of 1:10,000 for the lowermost 24.8 km of the Bandon Reach and 1:3,000 for the rest of the study area using the

Geographic Information System (GIS) programs ESRI ArcGIS™ 9.3.1 and 10.0.3. Although bars were not classified according to grain size (or vegetation or habitat types), field observations made during July 2010 indicated that most bars in the Powers, Broadbent, and Myrtle Point Reaches were composed of rounded gravel and finer particles with bar texture generally fining toward the head of tide at RKM 63.2. Bars were primarily composed of coarse, subangular basalt clasts in the Bridge Reach and sand and fine grain particles in the Gravelford and Bandon Reaches. The Bandon Reach also contains mud flats and tidal marshes near the Coquille River mouth. While most of the mapped bars had little to no vegetation, some bars included small areas that were partly or wholly covered by grasses, shrubs, and (to a lesser extent) mature trees. The delineation of bars, channel centerlines, and wetted channel edges was repeatedly verified to ensure consistent delineation of features among years and throughout the study area following the protocol of Wallick and others (2011).

Our mapping and change analysis relied on vertical aerial photographs obtained from various sources (table 4). Photographs from 2005 and 2009 were taken by the USDA's NAIP program. Scanned copies of black and white photographs taken in 1939 and 1967 were acquired from the University of Oregon Map and Aerial Photography Library and georeferenced for this study using techniques similar to Wallick and others (2011). Because the 1939 aerial photographs covered only the Powers Reach between RKM 108.1 and 96.9, repeat feature delineation was done for only this segment of the Powers Reach (fig. 8). Streamflows were generally lowest during the 2005 photography (1.6 m^3/s) and slightly greater during the collection of the 2009 (approximately 1.6–2.5 m^3/s) and 1939 (2.7–4.1 m^3/s) photography (table 10). Streamflow during the 1967 photography was substantially greater than during the other photographic activities and ranged from 7.3 to 26.1 m^3/s. These streamflow differences between the photographs likely affect the year to year comparisons of mapped features.

The quality of underlying photographs and errors introduced by georectified and digitizing processes are three of many potential sources of uncertainty in digital channel maps (Gurnell, 1997; Mount and Louis, 2005; Hughes and others, 2006; Walter and Tullos, 2009). Aerial photographs of the Coquille River study area were of sufficient resolution and generally free of glare and shadow to enable precise mapping. The 1939 and 1967 photographs were georectified with a minimum of eight ground-control points concentrated near the main channel and rectified with a second-order polynomial transformation. The total root mean square error (RMSE) values of the rectified photographs from 1939 and 1967 indicated that horizontal-position uncertainties associated with the georectification process ranged from 1.4 to 6.4 m for individual photographs, but averaged 3.2 m for the 1939 photographs and 3.4 m for the 1967 photographs. Because control points were concentrated near the channel, error associated with mapped features along channel corridor should be lower than the total RMSE values for the entire photograph.

Table 10. Stream discharge for the aerial and orthophotographs used for repeat bar and channel feature delineation in the Coquille River study area, southwestern Oregon.

[m³/s, cubic meter per second; --, same as main discharge; UO, University of Oregon; USACE, U.S. Army Corps of Engineers; USGS, U.S. Geological Survey]

Year	Reach	Flight dates	USGS gaging station used to determine discharge on day of photograph collection	Mean daily discharge (m³/s)		
				Minimum	Maximum	Main[1]
1939[2]	Powers	5/5	South Fork at Powers (14325000)	--	--	2.7
	Broadbent	5/5	South Fork at Powers (14325000)	--	--	2.7
	Myrtle Point	5/5	South Fork at Powers (14325000)	--	--	2.7
	Bandon	5/5	South Fork at Powers (14325000)	--	--	2.7
	Bridge	5/5	Middle Fork near Myrtle Point (14326500)	--	--	2.5
	Gravelford	5/5	North Fork near Myrtle Point (14327000)	--	--	4.1
1967	Powers	5/8; 5/25	South Fork at Powers (14325000)	7.3	26.1	7.3, 26.1
	Broadbent	5/8; 5/25	South Fork at Powers (14325000)	7.3	26.1	26.1
	Myrtle Point	5/8; 5/25	South Fork at Powers (14325000)	7.3	26.1	26.1
	Bandon	5/25; 8/5	South Fork at Powers (14325000)	0.9	7.3	7.3
	Bridge	5/8; 5/19; 5/25	South Fork at Powers (14325000)[3]	7.3	26.1	26.1
	Gravelford	5/8	North Fork near Myrtle Point (14327000)	--	--	18.8
2005	Powers	7/17; 7/19; 8/5	South Fork at Powers (14325000)	0.9	1.6	1.6
	All other reaches	7/17	South Fork at Powers (14325000)[3,4]	--	--	1.6
2009	Powers	6/22; 7/15	South Fork at Powers (14325000)	1.6	2.5	1.6, 2.5
	Broadbent	6/18; 7/15	South Fork at Powers (14325000)	1.6	2.3	1.6, 2.3
	Myrtle Point	6/18; 7/15	South Fork at Powers (14325000)	1.6	2.3	1.6, 2.3
	Bandon	6/17/; 6/18; 7/15	South Fork at Powers (14325000)	1.6	2.4	2.3
	Bridge	6/22; 7/15	South Fork at Powers (14325000)[3]	1.6	2.5	1.6
	Gravelford	6/22; 7/15	South Fork at Powers (14325000)[4]	1.6	2.5	1.6, 2.5

[1] Main discharge is the streamflow when most of the reach was photographed. Two discharge values are provided when areal coverages were approximately equal for photograph collection dates.

[2] Dates derived from 1939 photographs at USACE library in Portland, Oregon

[3] USGS streamflow-gaging station on Middle Fork Coquille River near Myrtle Point, Oregon (14326500) not operational

[4] USGS streamflow-gaging station on North Fork Coquille River near Myrtle Point, Oregon (14327000) not operational

Distribution and Area of Bars, 2009

In 2009, the total area of bars delineated along the Coquille River and its forks within the study area was 2,896,020 m^2 (table 11). Unit bar area, or the total area of bars per meter of channel length (m^2/m), was 21.0 m^2/m for all reaches (table 12). The tidal Bandon Reach had the greatest unit bar area for an individual reach (39.2 m^2/m), with extensive bars mapped in the lower 10 km (table 12). In the fluvial reaches, unit bar area ranged from 0.4 m^2/m in the Gravelford Reach to 12.6 m^2/m in the Powers Reach (table 12). Unit bar area values for fluvial reaches in the Coquille River basin are generally less than those reported for fluvial reaches in the bedrock-dominated Umpqua River basin (5.0–17.6 m^2/m from 2005 orthophotographs; Wallick and others, 2011) and substantially less than some values reported for fluvial or predominately fluvial reaches in the Hunter Creek basin (19.1 and 19.7 m^2/m from 2009 orthophotographs; Jones and others, 2011) and in the Rogue (10.6–63.1 m^2/m from 2009 orthophotographs; Jones and others, 2012), Applegate (4.3 and 71.5 m^2/m from 2009 orthophotographs; Jones and others, 2012), Illinois (91.8 m^2/m from 2009 photographs; Jones and others, 2012), and Chetco (9.3–77.5 m^2/m from 2005 orthophotographs; Wallick and others, 2010) River basins.

Examination of the bars delineated from the 2009 photographs (fig. 21A–C) shows that the location, abundance, and size of bars in fluvial reaches are mainly dictated by interrelated factors such as channel slope (fig. 3A–C) and confinement, which owe to factors such as valley physiography, the associated increase in floodplain width (fig. 3A–C) as the river approaches its mouth, and anthropogenic modifications including dikes and levees. As shown in figure 21A–C and table 11, bar area is substantially less in the Bridge and Gravelford Reaches on the Middle and North Forks of the Coquille River, respectively (figs. 12 and 13) and in the confined segments in the Powers (such as RKM 103.6–100.6; fig. 8), Broadbent (such as RKM 86.8–83.2; fig. 9), and Myrtle Point (such as RKM 66.2–64.8; fig. 10) Reaches on the South Fork Coquille River. Conversely, the greatest areal coverage of bars are in the unconfined segments of the Powers (such as RKM 115.4–103.6; fig. 8) and Broadbent (such as RKM 93, 88–87, and 73; fig. 9) Reaches.

The distribution of bars in the fluvial reaches also indicates key sources of gravel to the Coquille River. The greater area of bars in the reaches along the South Fork Coquille River relative to the reaches on the Middle and North Forks of the Coquille River indicates that the South Fork Coquille River basin is a primary source of gravel to the river network. Gravel production from the South Fork Coquille River is consistent with its situation as a high-relief basin draining the Klamath Mountains geologic province (fig. 1). The increase in bar area along the lower 3 km of the Bridge Reach (fig. 21B) likely reflects the river's cutting through an outcrop of Coast Range volcanic rocks, which produce much more competent material than the Coast Range sedimentary rocks that dominate much of the Middle Fork Coquille River basin (fig. 1).

The tidally influenced Bandon Reach has by far the greatest bar area, ranging from bars consisting of sand and finer particle sizes near the reach's upstream boundary to extensive mud flats and tidal wetlands in the reach's lowermost 15 km. Bar area is greatest near the Coquille River mouth (fig. 21A), corresponding with the increase in floodplain width (fig. 3A). The marked decline in channel gradient near the confluence of the South and North Forks of the Coquille River (RKM 58.5) likely promotes the deposition of coarse sediment load as well as suspended sediment loads transported from steeper and more confined upstream sections (figs. 2; and 3A–C), leading to bars in the uppermost Bandon Reach being composed of much finer material than bars in upstream reaches.

Table 11. Repeat bar attribute data as delineated from photographs taken in 1939, 1967, 2005, and 2009 for the Coquille River study area, southwestern Oregon.

[m², square meter; %, percent]

Reach	Bar area (m²)					Number of bars					Average bar area (m²)				
	1939	1967	2005	2009	Net % change	1939	1967	2005	2009	Net % change	1939	1967	2005	2009	Net % change
Powers[1]	184,640	72,040	130,010	140,530	-23.9	64	49	55	49	-23.4	2,890	1,470	2,360	2,870	-0.6
Broadbent	631,880	327,940	329,790	349,970	-44.6	122	77	128	134	9.8	5,180	4,260	2,580	2,610	-49.6
Myrtle Point	49,710	26,090	55,200	63,460	27.6	22	15	20	29	31.8	2,260	1,740	2,760	2,190	-3.2
Bandon	1,773,770	1,792,440	2,227,730	2,295,930	29.4	23	40	21	47	104.3	77,120	44,810	106,080	48,850	-36.7
Bridge	89,090	85,630	51,780	39,770	-55.4	62	42	36	26	-58.1	1,440	2,040	1,440	1,530	6.4
Gravelford	13,620	11,220	7,550	6,370	-53.2	18	7	10	8	-55.6	760	1,600	750	800	5.3
All reaches	2,742,710	2,315,350	2,802,050	2,896,020	5.6	311	230	270	293	-5.8	8,820	10,070	10,380	9,880	12.1
Tidal reaches[2]	1,823,480	1,818,530	2,282,920	2,359,390	29.4	45	55	41	76	68.9	40,520	33,060	55,680	31,040	-23.4
Fluvial reaches[3]	919,230	496,820	519,120	536,630	-41.6	266	175	229	217	-18.4	3,460	2,840	2,270	2,470	-28.4

[1] Repeat attribute data compiled for RKM 108.1–96.9

[2] Myrtle Point and Bandon Reaches

[3] Powers, Broadbent, Bridge, and Gravelford Reaches

Table 12. Repeat unit bar area data as delineated from photographs taken in 1939, 1967, 2005, and 2009 for the Coquille River study area, southwestern Oregon.

[m^2, square meter; %, percent]

Reach	Unit bar area (bar area per meter of channel; m²/m)				
	1939	1967	2005	2009	Net % change
Powers[1]	16.5	6.5	11.6	12.6	-23.9
Broadbent	20.6	10.9	10.8	11.4	-44.6
Myrtle Point	6.6	3.5	7.2	8.3	26.0
Bandon	30.4	30.8	38.1	39.2	28.9
Bridge	5.8	5.6	3.4	2.6	-55.6
Gravelford	0.9	0.8	0.5	0.4	-53.3
All reaches[2]	19.9	16.9	20.3	21.0	5.3
Tidal reaches[2,3]	27.7	27.7	34.6	35.6	28.7
Fluvial reaches[2,4]	12.8	7.0	7.2	7.5	-41.7

[1] Repeat attribute data compiled for RKM 108.1–96.9

[2] Unit bar area calculated using cumulative bar area and length for specified reaches

[3] Myrtle Point and Bandon Reaches

[4] Powers, Broadbent, Bridge, and Gravelford Reaches

The mapping of bars from photographs dating 1939 to 2009 shows that total bar area decreased in the fluvial reaches, but increased in the tidal reaches (table 11; fig. 22A). Along the South Fork Coquille River, total bar area declined by 24 and 45 percent in the fluvial Powers and Broadbent Reaches, respectively. Total bar area in the fluvial Bridge and Gravelford Reaches of the Middle and North Forks of the Coquille River decreased by 55 and 53 percent, respectively. In contrast, total bar area increased by 26 and 29 percent in the tidal Myrtle Point and Bandon Reaches, respectively. Net changes in the repeat measurements of unit bar area were similar to the net changes in total bar area (table 12).

Net changes in the number (fig. 22B; table 11) and average area of bars (table 11) varied by reach from 1939 to 2009. Generally, the number of mapped bars declined for the Powers, Bridge, and Gravelford Reaches with bars remaining approximately the same average area or increasing slightly in area. In the Broadbent Reach, bars became more numerous, but diminished by nearly 50 percent in average area from 1939 and 2009 (table 11). Likewise, in the tidal Myrtle Point and Bandon Reaches, bars increased in number while decreasing in average area (table 11).

Results for Repeat Channel Centerline and Width Delineations, 1939–2009

Comparison of channel centerline length over time reveals that the length of the channel changed little for all reaches from 1939 to 2009 and that the greatest change was channel length increasing 1.3 percent, or 100 m, in the Myrtle Point Reach (fig. 22C; table 13). Despite the overall stability in channel length (as delineated for this study), specific areas with lateral channel shifting include RKM 107.6–105.4 in the Power Reach (fig. 23), RKM 94–93.4, 83.2–78.8, and 75–69.6 in the Broadbent Reach (figs. 24, 25, and 26), RKM 4.2 and 2–0 in the Bridge Reach (fig. 27), and RKM 4.2–4 in the Gravelford Reach (fig. 28). In all of these reaches, however, lateral movement of the channel centerline was less than 120 m.

Mapped wetted channel width is sensitive to the streamflow and tide levels at the time the photographs were taken. Nevertheless, from 1939 to 2009, the average wetted width of the channel increased in all reaches except the Bandon Reach (fig. 22D; table 13). In fluvial reaches, the net increases in average wetted width ranged from 1 m in the Powers and Bridge Reaches to 5 m in the Broadbent Reach. Because discharge was similar during the collection of the 1939 and 2009 photographs (table 10), these changes in average wetted width in the fluvial reaches may indicate actual channel widening, possibly in association with the loss of bar area. A more detailed delineation of the active channel width (instead of wetted channel width, which can be influenced by small streamflow or tide differences) may help better quantify possible changes in channel width for the fluvial study reaches and its relation to the extent and number of bars.

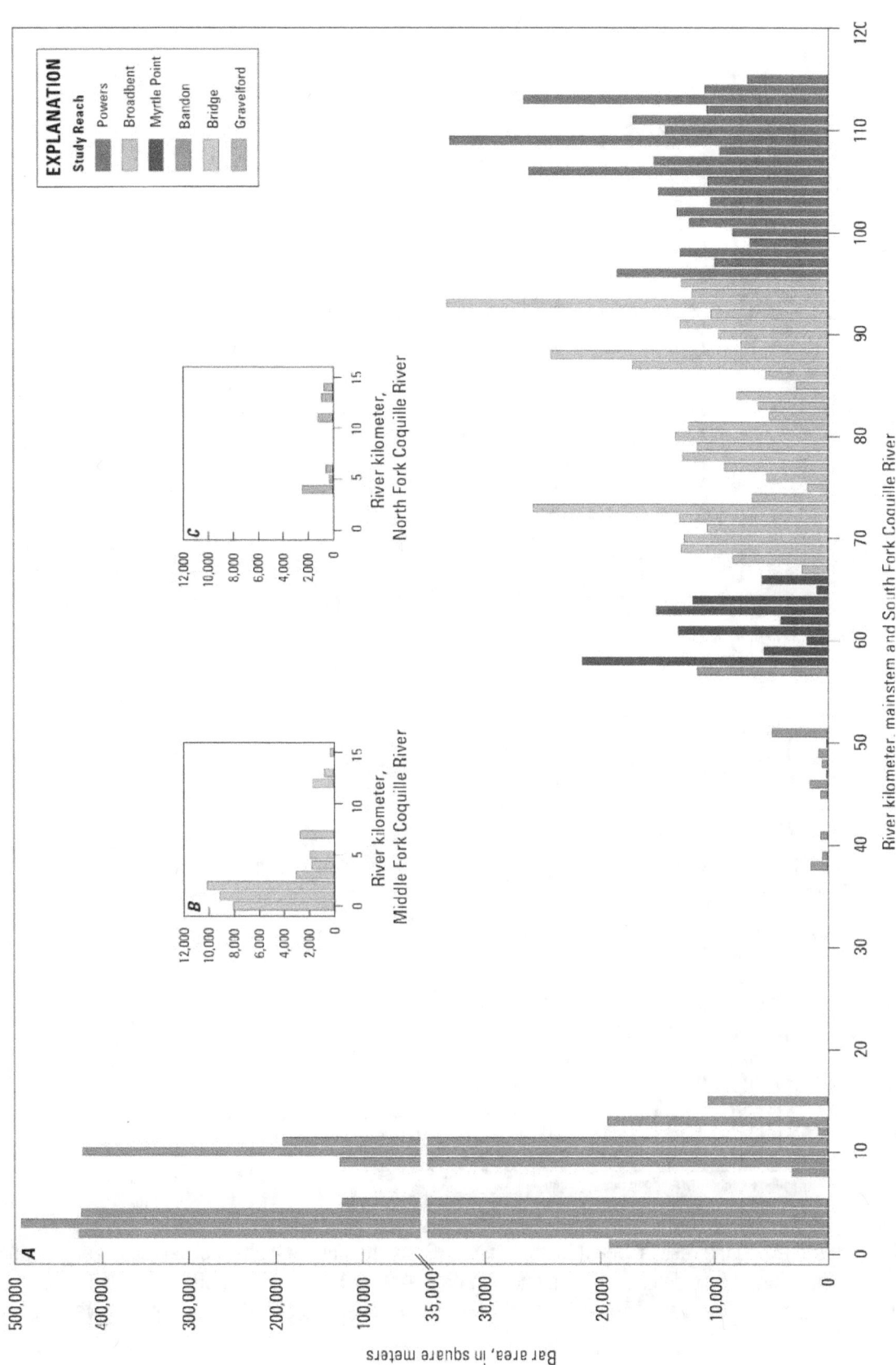

Figure 21. Graphs showing bar area by river kilometer as delineated from orthophotographs taken in 2009 for study reaches on the (A) South Fork and mainstem Coquille River, (B) Middle Fork Coquille River, and (C) North Fork Coquille River, southwestern Oregon. The upstream extent of the Powers Reach is RKM 115.4.

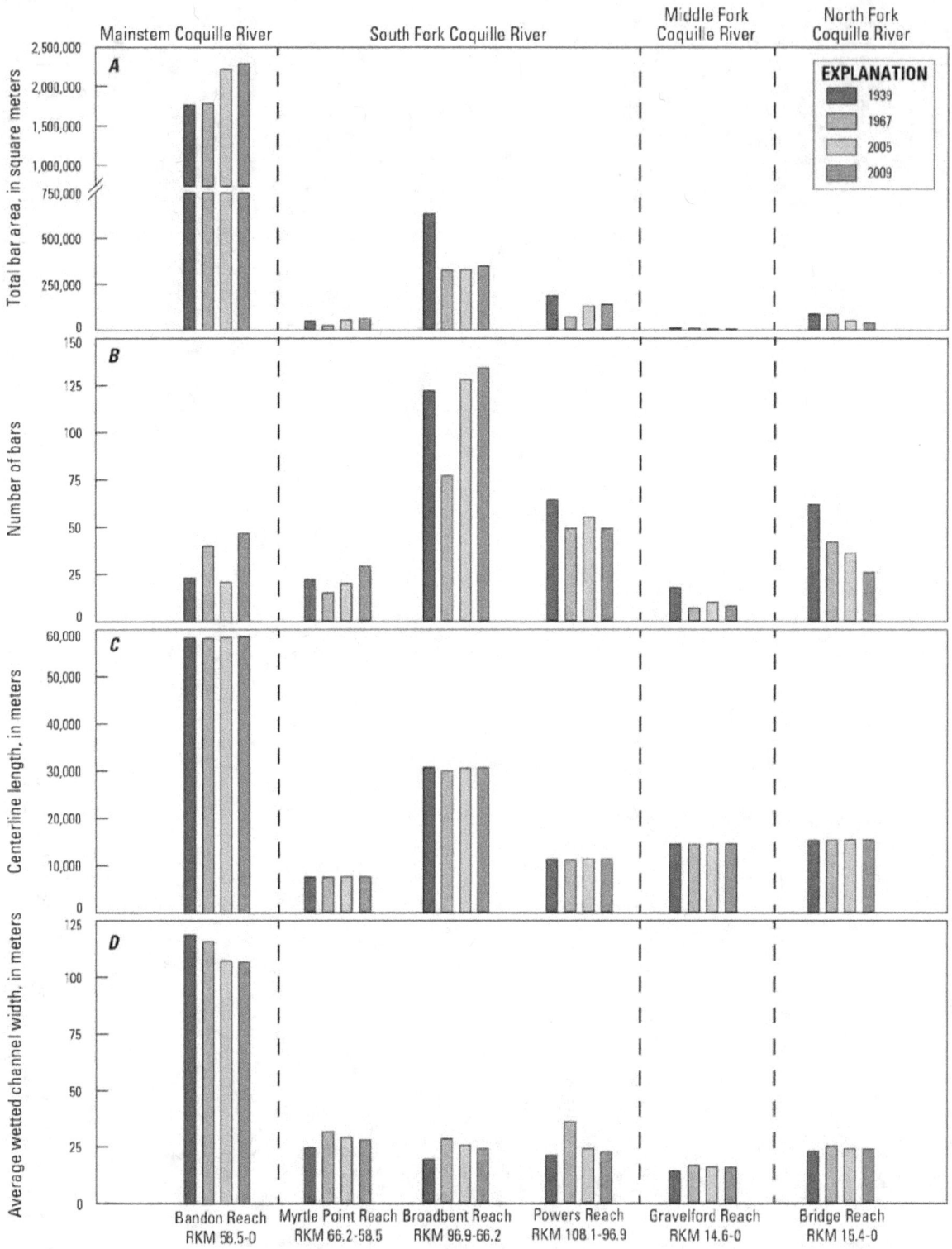

Figure 22. Graphs showing the results for (A) total bar area, (B) bar number, (C) channel centerline length, and (D) average wetted channel width as delineated from photographs taken in 1939, 1967, 2005, and 2009 for the study areas on the mainstem and North and Middle Forks of the Coquille River and South Fork Coquille River to RKM 108.1.

Table 13. Repeat channel feature data as delineated from photographs taken in 1939, 1967, 2005, and 2009 for the Coquille River study area, southwestern Oregon.

[m, meter; %, percent; RKM, river kilometer]

Reach	Centerline length (m)					Average wetted channel width (m)				
	1939	1967	2005	2009	Net % change	1939	1967	2005	2009	Net % change
Powers[1]	11,180	11,040	11,180	11,170	0.0	21	36	24	22	7.6
Broadbent	30,740	30,050	30,570	30,710	-0.1	19	29	26	24	24.6
Myrtle Point	7,580	7,530	7,640	7,680	1.3	25	31	29	28	14.0
Bandon	58,260	58,170	58,410	58,520	0.4	119	116	108	107	-9.9
Bridge	15,330	15,330	15,420	15,410	0.5	23	25	24	24	3.7
Gravelford	14,560	14,520	14,560	14,600	0.2	14	17	16	16	11.6
All reaches	137,650	136,640	137,770	138,090	0.3	60	60	60	60	-5.3
Tidal reaches[2]	65,840	65,710	66,050	66,200	0.5	108	106	99	98	-9.3
Fluvial reaches[3]	71,810	70,940	71,730	71,890	0.1	19	26	23	22	14.5

[1] Repeat attribute data compiled for RKM 108.1–96.9

[2] Myrtle Point and Bandon Reaches

[3] Powers, Broadbent, Bridge, and Gravelford Reaches

Discussion of Changes in Bar and Channel Features, 1939–2009

For the Powers and Broadbent Reaches on the South Fork Coquille River, the reductions in bar area were greatest from 1939 and 1967 (table 11, fig. 22A). Inspection of the photographs reveals that most of this apparent reduction owes to the higher streamflows of the 1967 photographs (table 10). Additional examination of the photographs, however, suggests that the net reduction in bar area between 1939 and 2009 is associated with changes in channel position and deposition patterns (such as RKM 107.4–105.8, fig. 23; RKM 83.2–78, fig. 24; RKM 74.8–71.6, fig. 25; RKM 95–93, fig. 26) and vegetation establishment on previously active bar surfaces (such as RKM 76.8; fig. 26). Also, some bar surfaces delineated from the 1939 photographs have been eroded laterally, becoming part of the wetted channel in 2009 (such as near RKM 108–107.8 and 106.8, fig. 23; RKM 82.8–82.2, 81.6–81.2, and 78.6–78.4, fig. 24). This lateral bar erosion is probably one cause of local increases in average wetted channel width (table 13).

As documented in the hazard maps by English and Coe (2011), segments of the South Fork Coquille River have shifted laterally in the past and are expected to shift in the future. From 1939 to 2009, the wetted channel has shifted laterally in the Powers Reach (such as near RKM 106.2 and 107.2, fig. 23). In the Broadbent Reach, lateral channel movement has lengthened some channel meanders, altering the extent and configuration of bars (figs. 24 and 25). At some dynamic channel bends, bar growth has likely resulted in the scour and erosion of banks on the opposite side of the river (such as near RKM 79, fig. 24; RKM 73.4, fig. 25). More nuanced conclusions regarding bank erosion processes in the Broadbent Reach will likely require detailed field measurements, hydraulic modeling, and a sediment budget to document trends in flow and sediment in relation to bank erosion in this dynamic section of the South Fork Coquille River.

Lateral channel movement, bar geometry changes, and vegetation establishment on bar surfaces were evident in the repeat delineation of bar and channel features near instream gravel mining sites on the South Fork Coquille River. For

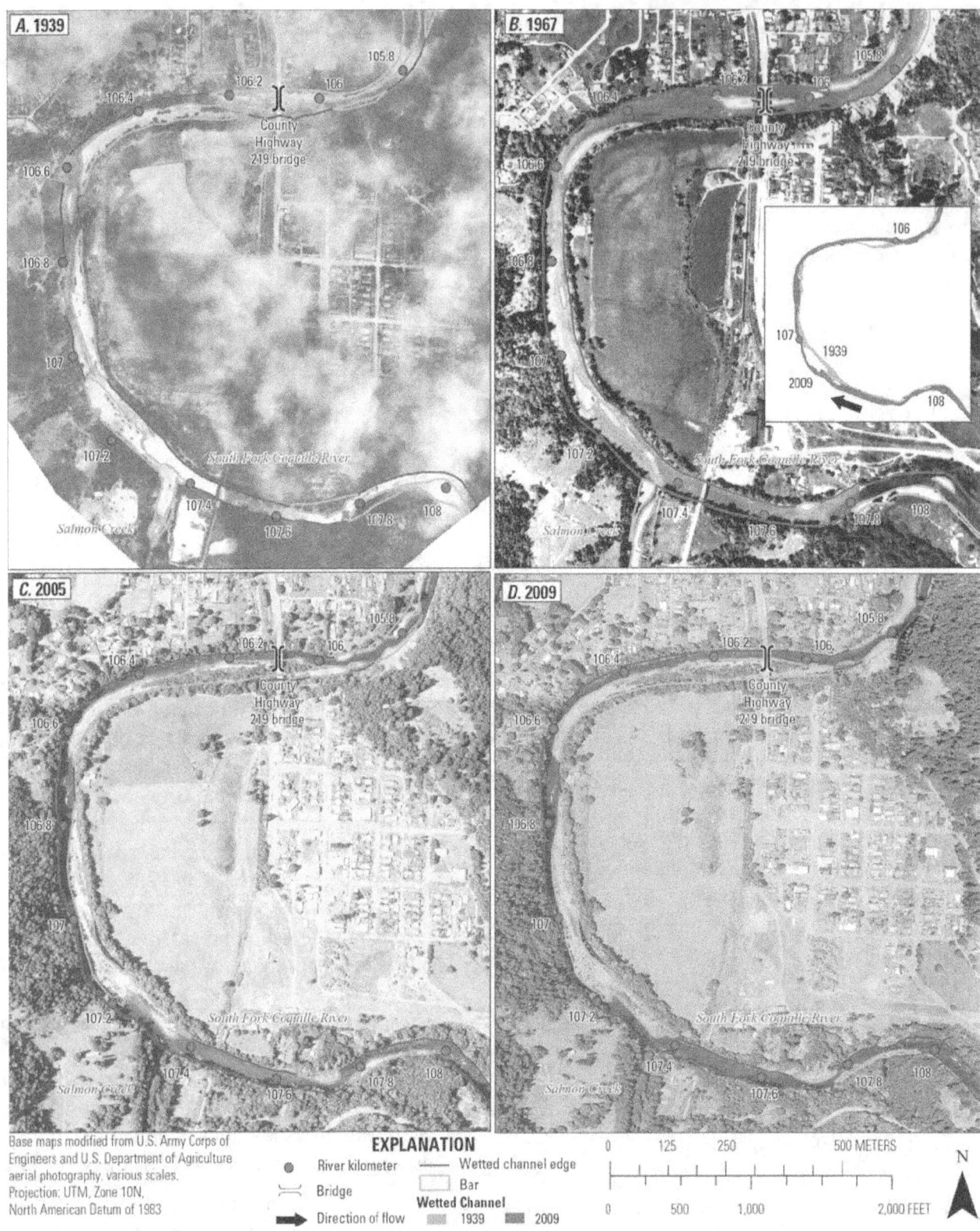

Figure 23. Images showing repeat bar and channel delineations, lateral channel shifting, and vegetation establishment on bars in a section of the Powers Reach on the South Fork Coquille River, southwestern Oregon.

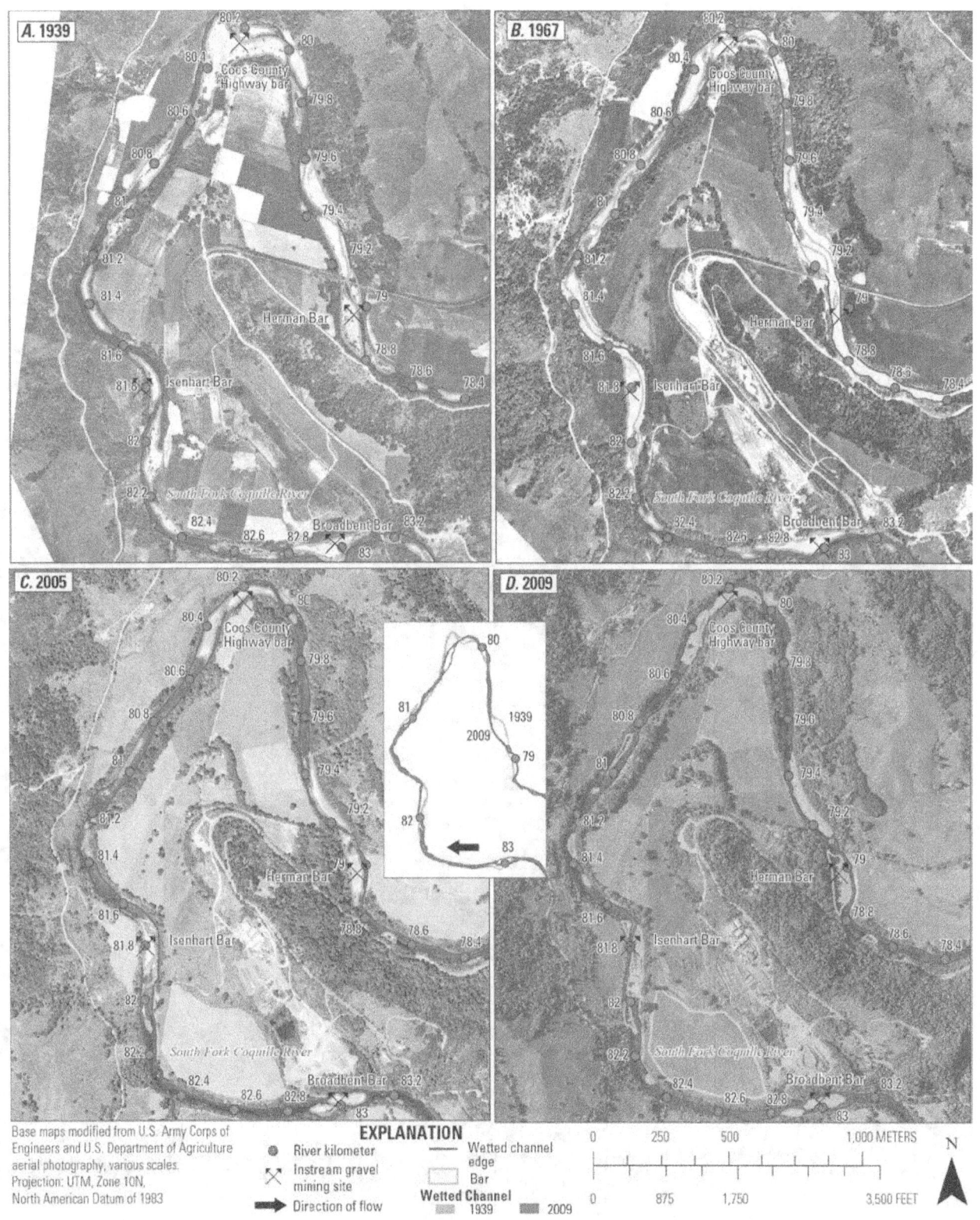

Figure 24. Images showing repeat bar and channel delineations, lateral channel movement, bank erosion, and other channel changes in the Broadbent Reach on the South Fork Coquille River near Warner, Oregon.

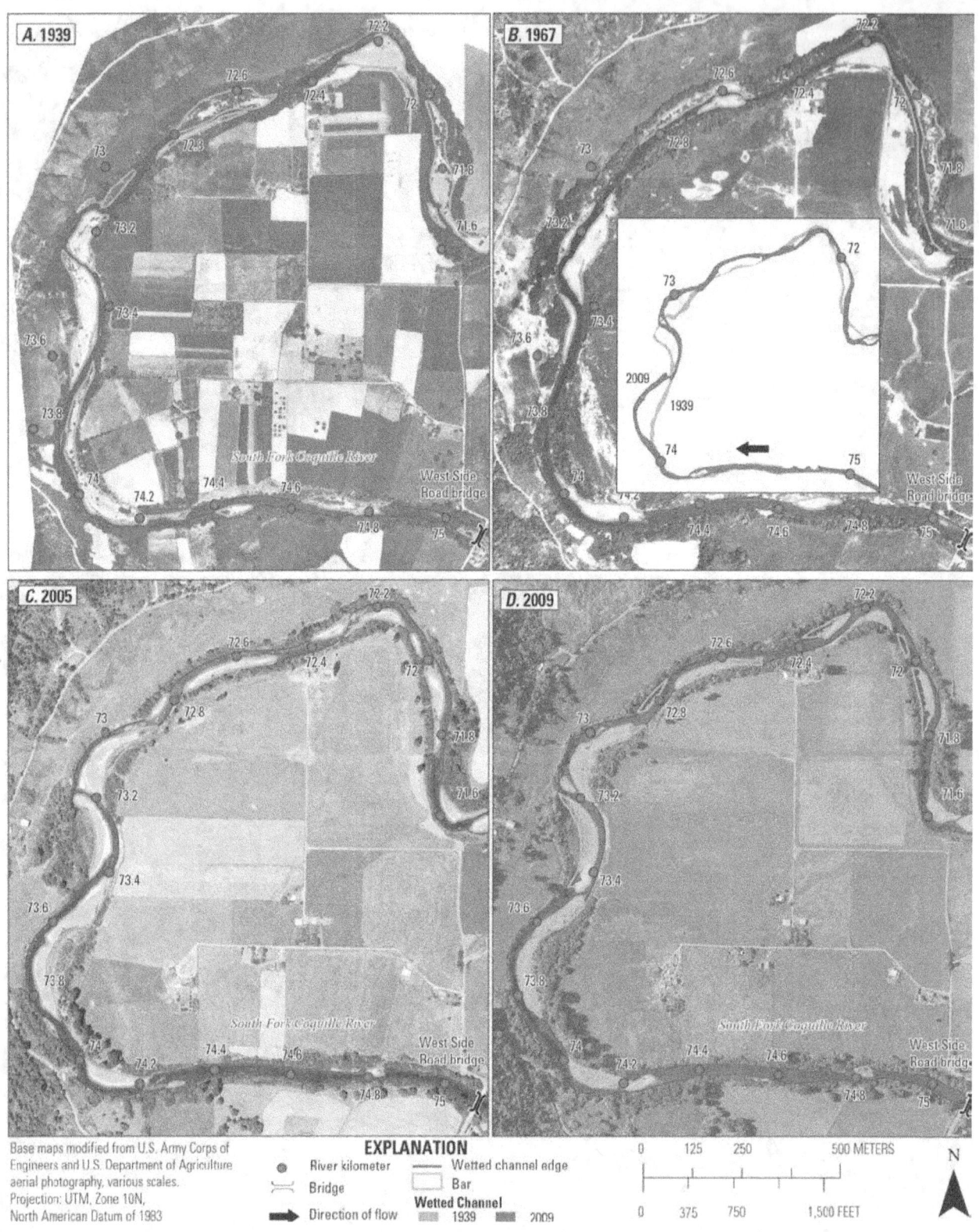

Figure 25. Images showing repeat bar and channel delineations, lateral channel movement, bank erosion, and other channel changes in the Broadbent Reach on the South Fork Coquille River near Broadbent, Oregon.

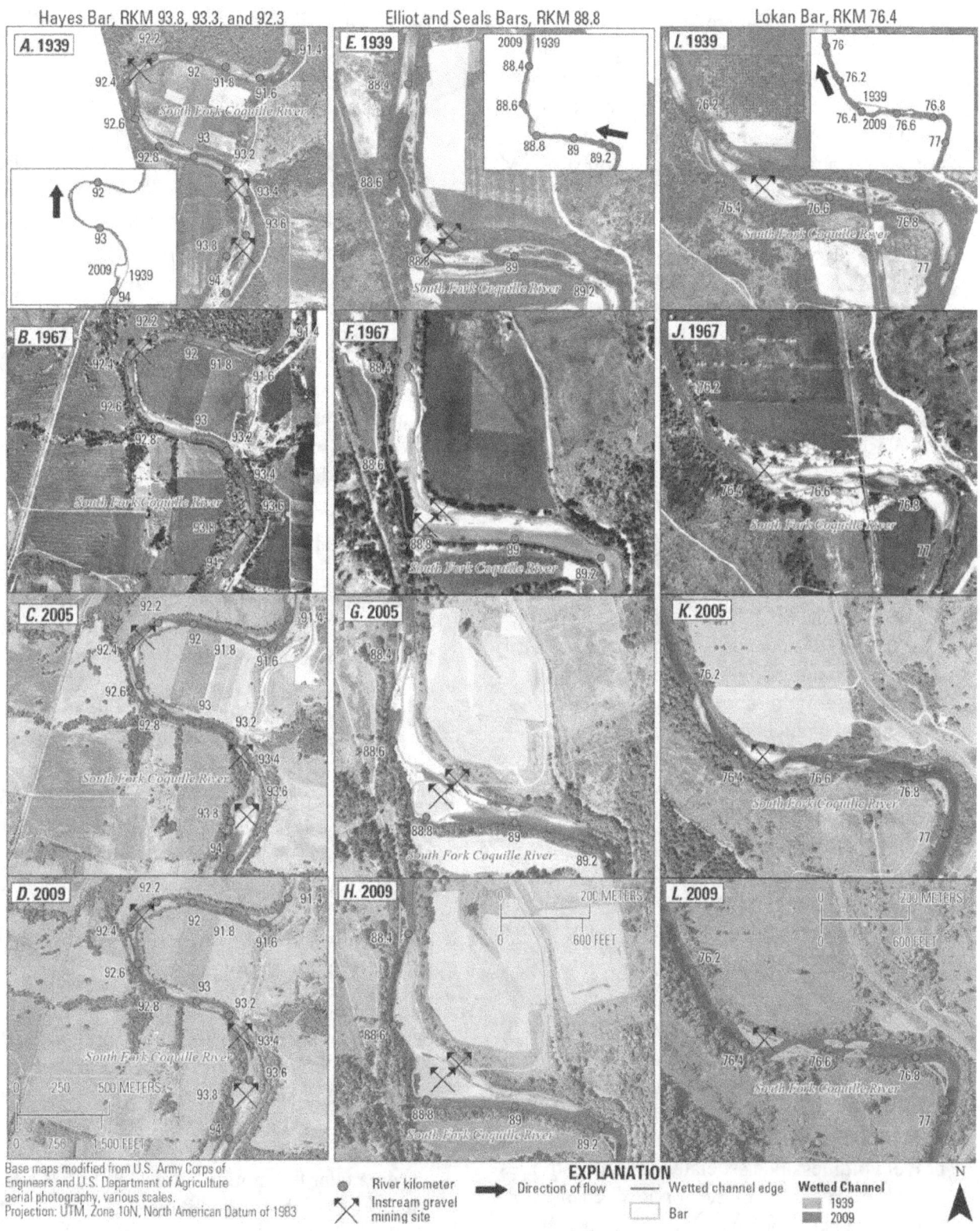

Figure 26. Images showing repeat bar and channel delineations for Hayes, Elliot/Seals, and Lokan Bars in the Broadbent Reach on the South Fork Coquille River, southwestern Oregon.

instance, at Hayes Bar (referred to as three sites at RKM 93.8, 93.3, and 92.3), the large bar on the west bank was stabilized by vegetation from 1939 to 1967, but then was partially eroded from 1967 to 2005 when the channel shifted westward following bar building on the east bank near RKM 93.8 (fig. 26). Downstream at the Elliot and Seals Bars (RKM 88.8), the channel has shifted toward the south bank at the bend, resulting in the conversion of the multiple bars into primarily one point bar with the Seals and Elliot Bars connected at low streamflow (fig. 26). Near Lokan Bar (RKM 76.4), the extent of bars has declined following the lateral migration of the channel at RKM 76.6-76.4 from 1939-1967 as well as vegetation establishment on multiple bars and an increase in wetted channel width near RKM 76.6 from 1967 to 2005 (fig. 26). Near Warner, Oregon (fig. 24), changes in the position of the channel have split Broadbent Bar (RKM 83) into two bars, reduced the area of Coos County Highway Bar (RKM 80.2), and eroded Isenhart Bar (RKM 81.8) with deposition occurring primarily on the east bank in 2009. Upstream and downstream of Herman Bar at RKM 79.0, four alternating channel bars are present along the channel in 1939 (fig. 24). Following changes owing to factors such as lateral channel movement and vegetation establishment, the channel flanking bars in this section have changed in distribution and extent and reduced in number from four to two bars. In particular, the erosion of the east bank opposite of the bar at RKM 79.0 has become more pronounced.

On the basis of this preliminary analysis, it is unclear how these changes in bar area and configuration may specifically relate to gravel mining activities. In the absence of gravel mining, the Broadbent Reach is likely dynamic, with active bar building and channel migration. Changes in gravel volumes and associated mining activities probably have some effects on local channel behavior and bar geometry; documenting such effects would require in-depth, comprehensive studies including hydrologic and sediment modeling of the South Fork Coquille River.

On the Middle and North Forks of the Coquille River, the greater than 50-percent net reductions in bar area from 1939 to 2009 were associated primarily with vegetation growth and subsequent stabilization of formerly unvegetated bar surfaces (fig. 27; fig. 28). In the Bridge Reach on the Middle Fork Coquille River, bars changed shape and increased slightly in area (such as RKM 1.8; fig. 27; table 11), possibly owing to lateral channel migration and changes in deposition patterns. The 1967 photographs of the Bridge Reach show evidence of scour and bank erosion, likely from the December 1964 flood (fig. 27). On the North Fork Coquille River, the net reduction in bar area is mainly from vegetation stabilizing banks, particularly in areas that were eroding and sloughing sediment into the channel in 1939 (fig. 28).

Unlike the fluvial reaches, the tidally affected Myrtle Point and Bandon Reaches exhibited net increases in total bar area between 1939 and 2009 (table 11; fig. 22A). Inspection of the aerial photographs indicates that the apparent initial decrease in bar area from 1939 to 1967 in the Myrtle Point Reach is mainly due to discharge differences between the photographs (table 10). A review of the 1967 photographs also reveals areas with scour (such as near RKM 62; fig. 29), possibly from the December 22, 1964, flood. From 1967 to 2005, the South Fork Coquille River shifted its position and eroded into some banks within the Myrtle Point Reach; some of this migration resulted in new bars such as those near RKM 62 and 64.6 (fig. 29).

In the Bandon Reach, bar area increased by 1 percent from 1939 to 1967 and then increased by 24 percent from 1967 to 2005. Substantial portions of the increase in bar area and some of the decrease in average wetted channel width (table 13) are likely associated with an increase in bar area near the mouth of the Coquille River (fig. 30). Based on a qualitative review of the USGS quadrangle and National Oceanic and Atmospheric Administration (NOAA) nautical

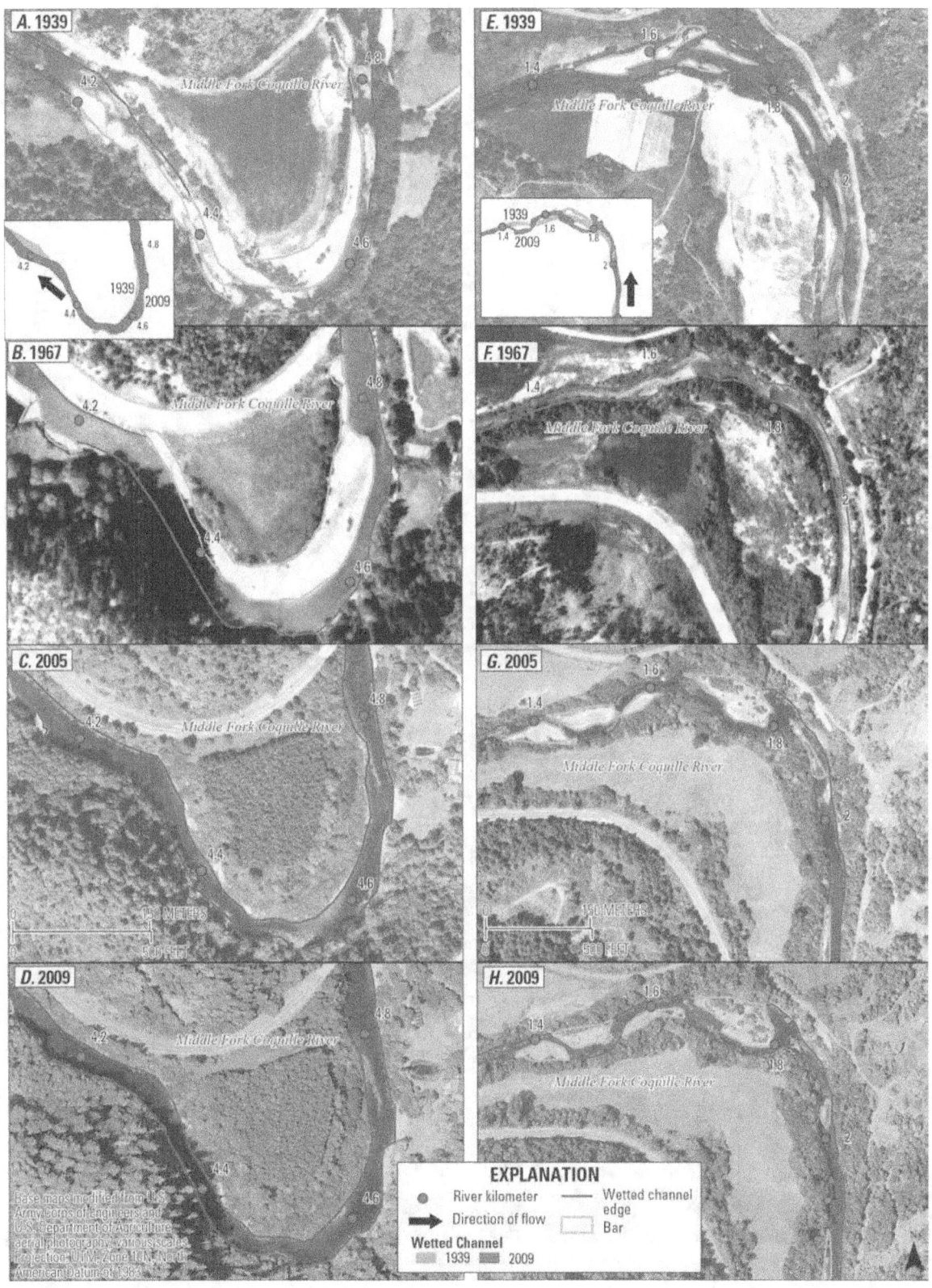

Figure 27. Images showing repeat bar and channel delineations, vegetation establishment, and lateral channel movement in the Bridge Reach on the Middle Fork Coquille River, southwestern Oregon.

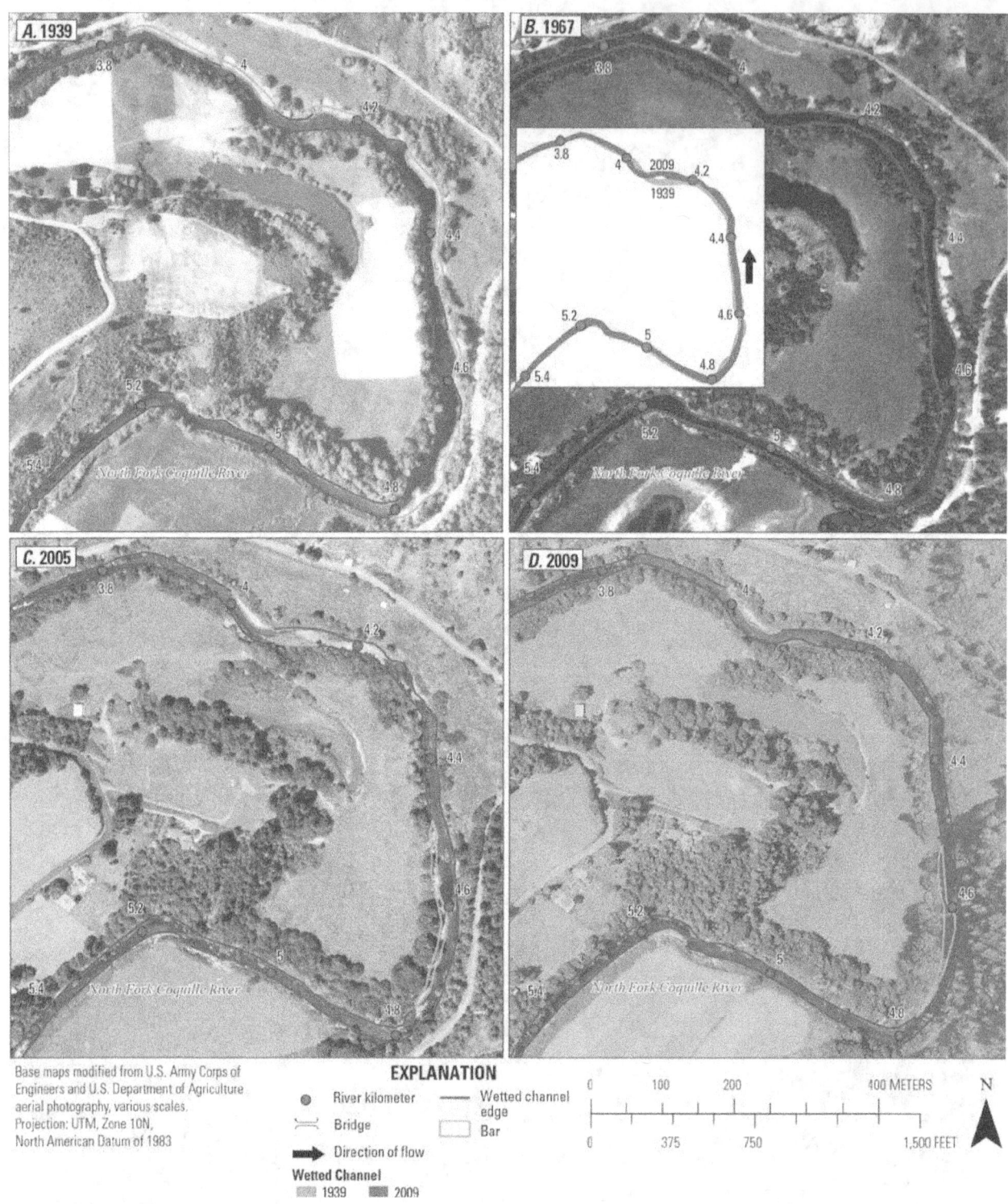

Figure 28. Images showing repeat bar and channel delineations and vegetation establishment in the Gravelford Reach on the North Fork Coquille River, southwestern Oregon.

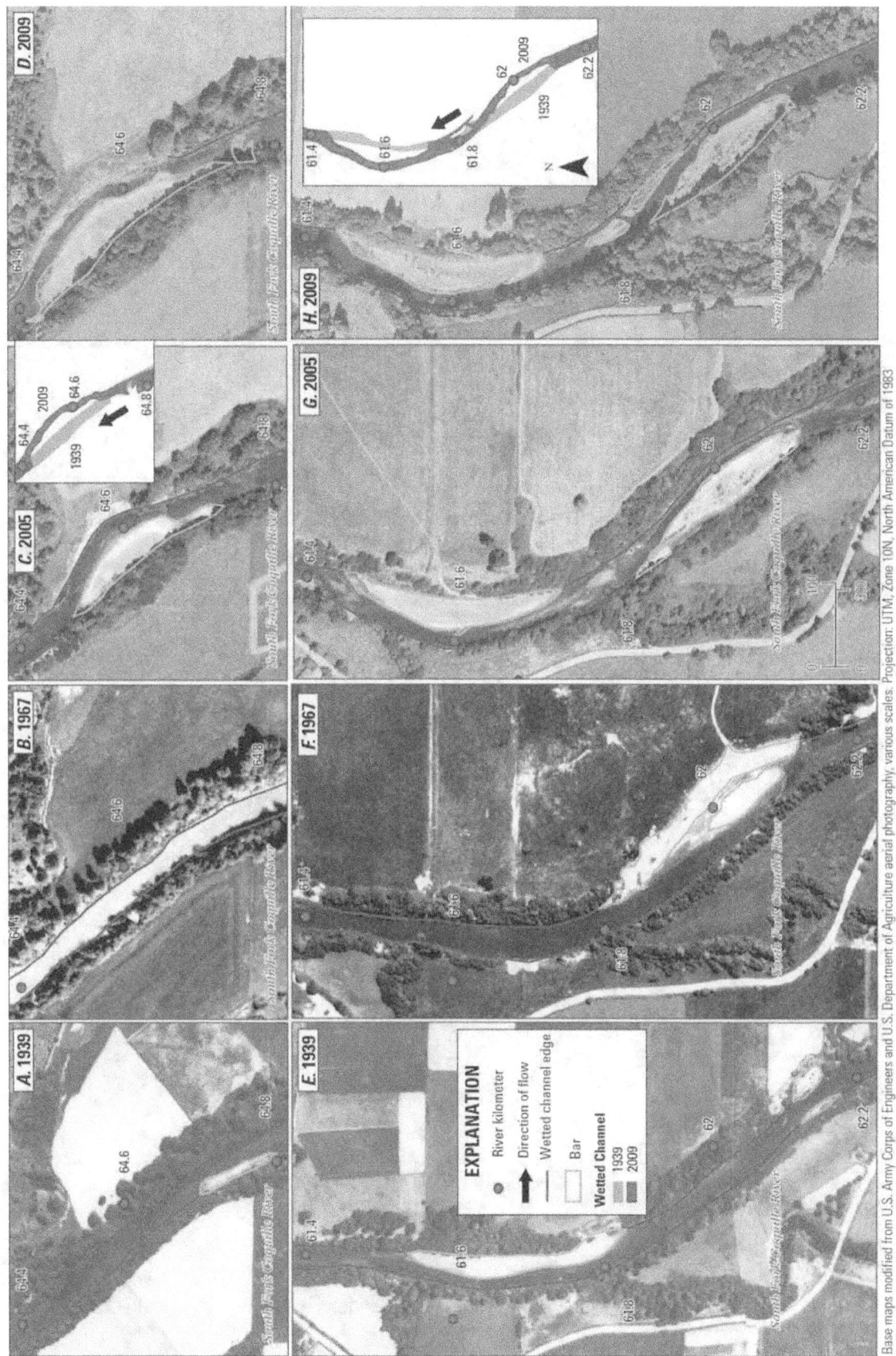

Base maps modified from U.S. Army Corps of Engineers and U.S. Department of Agriculture aerial photography, various scales. Projection: UTM, Zone 10N, North American Datum of 1983

Figure 29. Images showing repeat bar and channel delineations and lateral channel movement in the Myrtle Point Reach on the South Fork Coquille River, southwestern Oregon.

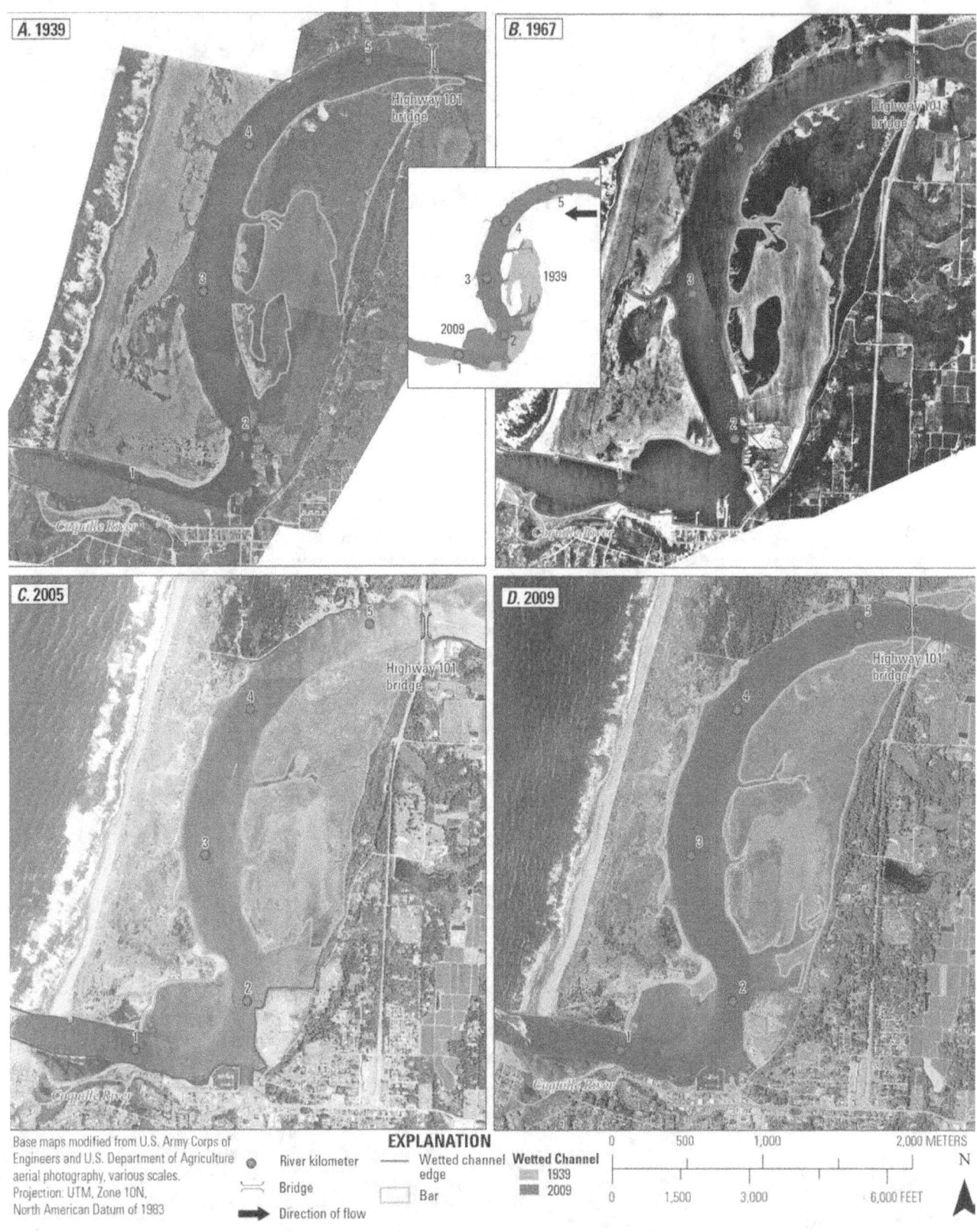

Figure 30. Images showing repeat bar and channel delineation in Bandon Reach near the mouth of the Coquille River, southwestern Oregon.

charts to the Coquille River entrance (table 5), differences in the mapping of the large tidal mudflat on the east side of the bay are likely associated with tide differences between the photographs. Other factors contributing to the increased bar area include possible sediment deposition from 1967 to 2005 and reductions in dredging volumes near the Coquille River mouth (fig. 6). Quantitative comparison of bathymetric surveys may be useful for assessing the potential changes in sediment deposition within the bay.

Farther upstream, in the upper 1.3 RKM of the Bandon Reach, the channel has contained larger bars since 1967 (fig. 31). Scour of vegetated surfaces, sediment deposition, and lateral channel movement (likely following the December 22, 1964, flood) are evident in the 1967 photographs. Since 1967, vegetation has become established, stabilizing some of the previously scoured bars.

Analyses of Bed-Material Particle Sizes

In July 2010, we measured surface particle size distributions at two bars and collected a subsurface bulk sample at one bar along the South Fork Coquille River. Surface and subsurface particle data were collected at Seals Bar (an active instream mining site at RKM 88.8, Broadbent Reach), whereas only surface particle data were collected at China Flat Bar (approximately 2.4 km upstream of the Powers Reach; fig. 1). These bars were selected on the basis of bar size, accessibility, and condition (such as little to no recent vehicle disturbance). To maintain consistency with other completed and ongoing bed-material studies (Wallick and others, 2010, Wallick and others, 2011, Jones and others, 2011, and Jones and others, 2012), we collected bed material data at a point bar (Seals Bar) and a lateral bar (China Flat Bar) likely formed by recent deposition events as indicated by the absence or minimal coverage of vegetation.

At the China Flat and Seals Bars, 200 surface particles were measured using a modified grid technique (Kondolf and others, 2003) and gravelometer measurement template (Federal Interagency Sediment Project US SAH-97 Gravelometer), which allows for the standardized measurement of sediment clasts greater than 2 mm in diameter. Diameter measurements of surface particles were taken at 0.3-m increments along two parallel 30-m tapes that were placed 1–2 m apart and parallel to the long axis of the bar. To support consistent intersite comparisons, the measurement transects were located at the bar apex (defined as the topographic high point along the upstream end of the bar) when possible. At China Flat Bar, measurement transects were located in a section of the bar that appeared active and representative of bar texture since the apex was obstructed by some vegetation. Measurements at Seals Bar were taken prior to that summer's gravel mining by the Knife River Corporation.

At the surface bed-material measurement transect at Seals Bar, we also sampled the subsurface bed material to evaluate particle size differences between surface and subsurface bed material (a measure of bar "armoring"). We removed approximately 1 m^2 of the bar-surface material, and then collected 72 kg of the bar-substrate material. This bulk sample then was dried and analyzed for ½-phi particle sizes by the USGS Sediment Laboratory in Vancouver, Washington.

At the two sites on the South Fork Coquille River, the median diameter (D_{50}) of surface particles varied from 78.0 mm at China Flat Bar slightly upstream of the study area to 48.8 mm at Seals Bar in the Broadbent Reach (table 14, fig. 32A–C). Bar-surface material was larger than bar-subsurface material at Seals Bar (table 14, fig. 32A). Differences in the sizes of surface and subsurface particles can be related to the balance between sediment supply and transport capacity, with the surface layer coarsening when the transport capacity of a river exceeds its supply of fine sediments (Dietrich and others, 1989; Buffington and Montgomery, 1999) as well as with the selective transport of bed material (Lisle, 1995). The armoring ratio, or ratio of the

71

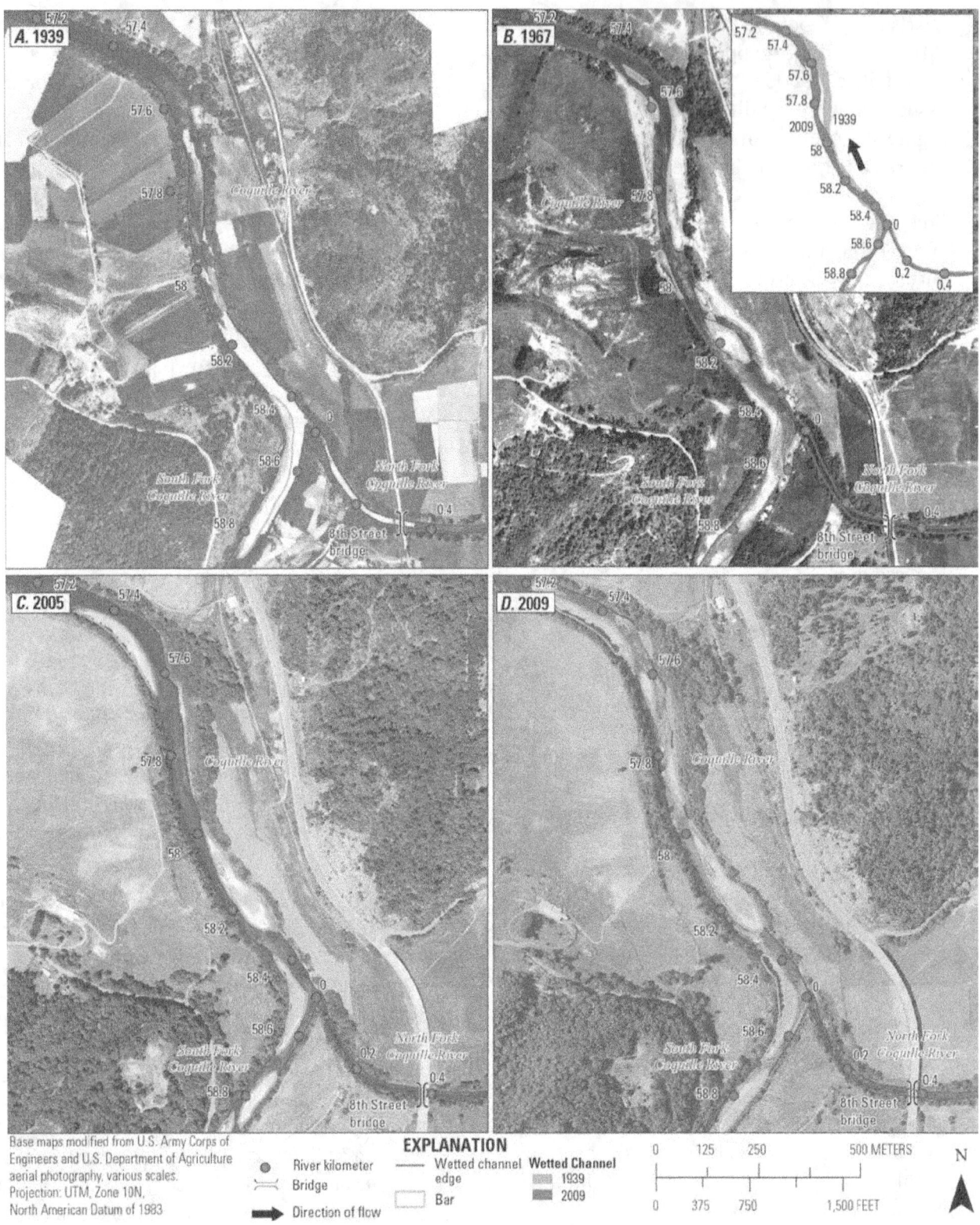

Figure 31. Images showing repeat bar and channel delineations and lateral channel movement in a section of the Bandon Reach on the Coquille River, southwestern Oregon.

median grain sizes (D_{50}) of the surface to subsurface layers, provides an indication of the degree of armoring. Armoring ratios are typically close to 1 (meaning surface and subsurface particles are of similar sizes) for rivers with a high sediment supply, and approach or exceed 2 for supply-limited rivers (Bunte and Abt, 2001). The armoring ratio for Seals Bar was 3.5, indicating sediment supply limitation at this site (table 14). For comparison, armoring ratios ranged from 0.99-4.73 in the Umpqua River basin (30 sites; Wallick and others, 2011), 1.2–3.4 in the Rogue River basin (7 sites, Jones and others, 2012), 1.38 to 2.09 in the Chetco River basin (3 sites; Wallick and others, 2010), and 0.97–1.5 in the Hunter Creek basin (2 sites; Jones and others, 2011). Because bar texture can vary tremendously between sites on gravel-bed rivers (as evident for Oregon coastal rivers), additional bed-material measurements within the study area would help refine assessments of transport and sediment-supply conditions and longitudinal bed-material trends for the Coquille River basin.

Discussion and Synthesis

On the basis of literature review, field observations, topographic analysis and delineation of bars and channels from multiple photographs, we defined a study area encompassing 145.4 km of the mainstem Coquille River and the lower parts of three main forks—the South, Middle, and North Forks of the Coquille River. Within the study area, the channels locally flow on or adjacent to bedrock as well as alluvial deposits. The active channels alternate between being confined and unconfined by flanking valley margins. Tide affects the entire mainstem Coquille River, South Fork Coquille River to RKM 63.2, and North Fork Coquille River to RKM 0.9. Within this study area, our analysis in conjunction with previous studies allows for a broad synthesis of channel and floodplain characteristics as well as overall bed-material transport conditions.

Table 14. Bed-material data collected in the Coquille River study area, southwestern Oregon.

[--, no data; km, kilometer; RKM, river kilometer; m, meter; mm, millimeter; D_{16}, 16th percentile diameter in mm; D_{50}, median diameter in mm; D_{84}, 84th percentile diameter in mm]

Bar	China Flat	Seals
Reach	--	Broadbent
Location	2.4 km upstream of Powers Reach	RKM 88.8
Northing (m)	4,736,738	4,756,715
Easting (m)	412,633	409,352
Surface particles		
D_{16} (mm)	23.0	16.4
D_{50} (mm)	78.0	48.8
D_{84} (mm)	267.1	90.0
Subsurface particles		
D_{16} (mm)	--	0.8
D_{50} (mm)	--	13.8
D_{84} (mm)	--	58.7
Armoring ratio	--	3.5

Spatial Variation in Channel Conditions

The full length of river within the study area can be divided into six study reaches based on topography and hydrology. The channels flow over alternating alluvial deposits and bedrock in the Powers (South Fork Coquille River) and Bridge (Middle Fork Coquille River) Reaches. Meanwhile, the channels flow over predominantly alluvial deposits in the Broadbent (South Fork Coquille River), Gravelford (North Fork Coquille River), Myrtle Point (mainstem Coquille River), and Bandon (mainstem Coquille River) Reaches.

As for many coastal rivers in Oregon, (for example, Wallick and others, 2011; Jones and others, 2011, 2012), valley confinement exerts a considerable control on the character of the tributaries and mainstem in the Coquille River basin. Generally, the confined segments contain fewer bars and have relatively stable planforms, whereas the unconfined segments have a greater number and area of bars and greater rates and magnitudes of lateral channel migration. Likewise, the geologic environment is a primary

Figure 32. Graph showing (A) size distributions of surface and subsurface particles and (B-C) photographs of measurement transects for two bed-material sampling sites along the South Fork Coquille River, southwestern Oregon. Surface size distributions were determined by measuring 200 clasts; subsurface size distribution was determined from a bulk sample taken below the armor layer.

factor controlling bed-material transport and channel morphology in the Coquille River and other Oregon coastal rivers. The South Fork Coquille River is the only tributary draining a substantial area of the Klamath Mountains geologic province. The metamorphic Mesozoic rocks of this geologic province combined with steep slopes and dense stream networks enhance the production and delivery of bed-material sediment, resulting in large bed-material fluxes as reported for the Chetco (Wallick and others, 2010) and Smith (MFG and others, 2006) Rivers and contributes to expansive bars and alluvial reaches on the Rogue and Illinois Rivers (Jones and others, 2012) and Hunter Creek (Jones and others, 2011).

The reaches along the South Fork Coquille River have the greatest unit bar area of the fluvial reaches, and have been historically subject to the most instream gravel mining. Of the two South Fork Coquille River reaches, however, the Broadbent Reach is likely the only fully alluvial reach as indicated by the much lower frequency of bedrock outcrops and greater measurements of total bar area in this reach compared to the Powers Reach (table 11; fig. 21A).

Unit bar area measurements were lowest for the Bridge and Gravelford Reaches on the Middle and North Forks of the Coquille River, which drain predominantly the sedimentary subdivision of the Coast Range geologic province. The local outcrop of the Coast Range volcanic rocks at the lower end of the Bridge Reach, however, apparently results in increased bed material as indicated by the greater frequency of bars in the lowermost 3 km of the Middle Fork Coquille River (figs. 12 and 21B).

The Bandon Reach (mainstem Coquille River), Myrtle Point Reach (South Fork Coquille River), and lower part of the Gravelford Reach (North Fork Coquille River) are tidally influenced river segments. In these reaches, gradients are much lower (fig. 3A,C) and substantial transport of gravel-sized bed material is unlikely. Bedload, and consequently most bed material in these reaches, is probably mostly sand and finer particles, much of which was probably transported as suspended load from the steeper upstream sections. The large bars in the lower 15 km of the Bandon reach are largely composed of this finer material. Additionally, the substantial length of river (about 64 km of channel, including all of the mainstem Coquille River and the lower parts of the South and North Forks of Coquille River) affected by tide reflects the Holocene sea-level rise and the consequent drowning of the lower Coquille River valley at a rate faster than it is being filled by coarse bed material (sand and gravel). This difference between sea-level rise and coarse sediment flux suggests that the Coquille River has relatively lower sand and gravel transport rates than other coastal rivers, such as the Rogue River (Jones and others 2012), Chetco River (Wallick and others, 2010), and Hunter Creek (Jones and others, 2011), where the tide affects less than 7 km of channel.

Temporal Trends in Channel and Bar Conditions

Patterns in the accumulation and texture of bed material logically relate to channel and valley physiography, hydrology, and geology. However, temporal trends in channel and bar conditions and their interpretation are more ambiguous and vary by reach. The interpretation of temporal trends is also hindered by the complex and locally intense land-use practices historically affecting the channels in the basin, including splash damming, dredging, and sand and gravel mining.

Multiple lines of evidence indicate that all reaches within the Coquille River study area have the potential for local vertical and lateral channel adjustments in response to changes in flow, sediment, and possibly riparian vegetation. In some sections, in-channel bedrock may locally constrain channel incision. The four fluvial reaches experienced a net reduction in bar area from 1939 to 2009, ranging from 24 percent in the Powers Reach to 55 percent in the Bridge Reach (figs. 23–fig. 31; table 11). In the Powers and Broadbent Reaches, the net loss in bar area is associated with multiple factors, including (1) channel planform changes and corresponding reconfigurations of deposition patterns, (2) vegetation establishment on bar surfaces thereby converting them to floodplain surfaces, and (3) lateral erosion of individual bars. In the Bridge and Gravelford Reaches, the reduction in bar area resulted from vegetation establishment on bar surfaces that were apparently unvegetated and eroding banks in 1939, as well as channel migration. These re-

sults are consistent with our findings of channel widening and local incision for each of the fluvial reaches based on channel width measurements (table 13), channel cross sections (table 9), and specific gage analysis for the Powers streamflow-gaging station (fig. 20). Particularly for the South Fork Coquille River, the channel appears to have both widened and deepened in many places since 1939. These findings are consistent with prior studies that noted incision and planform changes along the South Fork Coquille River (Florsheim and Williams, 1996; Clearwater Biostudies, Inc., 2003; English and Coe, 2011).

In contrast, bar area expanded in both tidal reaches and the channel narrowed in the Bandon Reach (tables 11 and 13). The net 28–29 percent increases in bar area owe to channel migration and deposition of newly formed bars in the Myrtle Point Reach and upper 1.2 RKM in the Bandon Reach as well as increases in mapped tidal flats near the Coquille River mouth. In the Bandon Reach, the channel has apparently narrowed by nearly 10 percent between 1939 and 2009. It is unclear if these trends in the tidal reaches are the consequence of some combination of (1) different streamflow and tide levels during the collection of aerial photographs, (2) increased loads of sand and silt from upstream sources, and (3) the long-term trajectory of sedimentary filling the extensive tidally affected section.

General Bed-Material Transport Conditions

Our observations of the spatial and temporal characteristics of the reaches support preliminary interpretations of bed-material transport conditions. Although the fluvial Powers, Bridge, and Gravelford Reaches are diverse in terms of bar area (fig. 21A–C; fig. 22A) and slope (fig. 3A–C), all three reaches have areas of in-channel bedrock or long segments with few bars (fig. 21A–C). These attributes indicate that the reaches are likely sediment supply limited in terms of bed material; that is, the transport capacity of the river generally exceeds its supply of bed material. In the Powers Reach on the South Fork Coquille River, high transport capacity is likely a result of the steeper gradient (0.0027 m/m; table 2) and locally confined valley that enables the South Fork Coquille River to transport bed material received from the upstream Klamath Mountain geologic province to the downstream and lower gradient Broadbent Reach. The Bridge Reach on the Middle Fork Coquille River also has a relatively high gradient (0.0015 m/m; table 3), contributing to its high transport capacity. Unlike the Powers Reach on the South Fork Coquille River, however, the Bridge Reach and upstream Middle Fork Coquille River are predominantly underlain by the highly erodible sedimentary subdivision of the Coast Range geologic province. This sedimentary subdivision produces large suspended sediment loads (Beschta, 1978) and bed-material clasts that disintegrate rapidly relative to those from other geologic provinces, such as the Klamath Mountains (Jones and others, 2010; Mangano and others, 2011), likely resulting in the limited supply of coarse sediment in this reach. The sediment-supply limitation of the Gravelford Reach on the North Fork Coquille River is likely attributable to its low transport capacity (gradient of 0.0003 m/m; table 3) in conjunction with presumably limited bed-material supply from the sedimentary Coast Range rocks that underlie most of this basin.

Contrasting with the Powers, Bridge, and Gravelford Reaches, the Broadbent Reach on the South Fork Coquille River is the only gravel-bed reach in the Coquille River basin where bed-material conditions may be transport-limited; meaning the bed-material flux through this reach is controlled by transport conditions rather than sediment supply. The nearly continuous alluvial channel of this reach and comparatively high unit bar area (table 12) are the primary reach characteristics supporting this inference.

Although the Broadbent Reach may be transport-limited, changes in recent decades may be shifting the reach toward supply limitation. In particular, the coarse surface texture and armoring ratio of 3.5 at Seals Bar (table 14), historically diminishing bar areas (fig. 22A; table 11), and local channel incision (table 9) are evidence of

such a trend. The isolated exposures of in-channel bedrock are also consistent with a shift toward supply limitation. As suggested by Florsheim and Williams (1996), historical sediment fluxes to this reach were possibly greater as a result of log drives, splash damming, and timber harvesting in the mid-19th to mid-20th centuries. Additionally, instream gravel mining over the last several decades has reduced the volume of bed-material moving through the reach (tables 6–8). Regardless of the current state of the balance between transport capacity and sediment supply in the Broadbent Reach, this reach is likely to be the most responsive of the four fluvial reaches to watershed conditions affecting sand and gravel supply and transport because of its low gradient, relatively unconfined floodplain, and location downstream of the gravel-producing Klamath Mountains geologic province.

Both tidal reaches are transport limited because of their low gradients. Bed material supplied to the Myrtle Point and Bandon Reaches, however, is primarily sand and finer materials. As illustrated by the historical descriptions of channel conditions and management actions intended to maintain a navigable channel, these reaches will be most susceptible to watershed conditions affecting the supply and transport of fine sediment.

Outstanding Issues and Possible Approaches

This reconnaissance-level study provides a framework and baseline information for understanding bed-material transport in the Coquille River basin. Future efforts addressing data gaps could greatly refine the understanding of historical and ongoing bed-material transport processes and their effects on channel morphology. Many of these approaches (as outlined below) could focus on individual reaches. Additionally, such information would provide a solid basis for evaluating future hydrologic and geomorphic changes in the basin.

Streamflow Data

Understanding and predicting bed-material transport require high-quality streamflow information, particularly for peak flows. As of 2011, no streamflow-gaging station is operated that measures the streamflow of the Middle or North Fork of the Coquille River. Such hydrologic data would be required by most approaches used to quantify sediment supplied to the Bridge or Gravelford Reaches or for the mainstem Bandon Reach in the continued absence of mainstem streamflow-gaging stations downstream of the North Fork Coquille River. The most accurate approach for obtaining such information would be to expand the gaging station network to include additional stations. Mean daily streamflow measured at the new stations could then be used to estimate annual sediment fluxes for the period of record and shorter time periods (such as water years) using methods outlined in Wallick and others (2010) and employed in Wallick and O'Connor (2011). An alternative approach (that is less costly but with greater uncertainties) would be to apply regional regression equations to estimate discharge for a range of flow events for specific locations. However, an operational gage would be the optimal location for sampling bedload and later estimating sediment flux.

Bed-Material Transport Rates and Sediment Budget

Understanding the possible effects of instream gravel mining on channel condition and longitudinal and temporal changes in bed material requires an accounting of sediment inputs from upstream and lateral sources as well as sediment losses due to particle attrition, transport, and storage. Such information would support an assessment of the volumes of gravel mined from the system by ongoing and past mining activities relative to gravel delivered to the study area. Developing a sediment budget may include the following components:

1. Estimate sediment flux using published bed-load transport equations following the approach used by Wallick and others (2010, 2011) for the Chetco and Umpqua Rivers. This approach could be used with most confidence in the reaches where bed-material transport is likely transport-limited, such as the Broadbent Reach. Similar to the analysis by Wallick and others (2010) for the Chetco River, such analyses would be best performed by developing a hydraulic model for the reach of interest in conjunction with systematic measurements of bed-material size. Existing data, including the LiDAR survey for most of the Powers Reach and entire Broadbent Reach, and discharge data from the Powers streamflow-gaging station in conjunction with a future bathymetric study of streambed topography, would support this approach.

2. Perform empirical GIS-based sediment yield analyses, factoring in sediment production, delivery to channels, and in-channel attrition. This approach would be similar to that applied for the Umpqua River basin (Wallick and others, 2011). While such an analysis could focus on specific reaches regardless of their alluvial or bedrock character, it would require analysis of their entire contributing area. Such analyses would be bolstered by assessments of bed-material composition, thereby confirming the source areas for bed-material delivered to the Coquille River.

3. Make direct measurements of bedload transport to verify equations for bedload transport and estimate actual bedload fluxes. Possible locations for bedload measurements on the South Fork Coquille River are the China Flat bridge (approximately 2.4 km upstream of study area) and the Gaylord Road bridge (Broadbent Reach, RKM 89.4). Ideally, such measurements would be made at a site of continuous discharge measurement; however, the Powers USGS streamflow-gaging station is not an ideal location for making bedload measurements because measurements would have to be made from either the station's cableway or the downstream two-lane bridge with a relatively high traffic load.

4. Estimate sediment flux based on mapped changes in bar area over specific temporal intervals in a manner similar to the morphological approach used on the Chetco River by Wallick and others (2010). Ideally, this approach would use LiDAR or other high-resolution topographic data from two time periods to directly calculate volumetric change in sediment storage. This method, however, can also be implemented using sequential aerial photographs along with the single available LiDAR survey. Like the analysis of bed-material transport using established transport capacity relationships (described above), this approach is best applied in alluvial reaches. Despite the inherent uncertainties associated with this type of analysis (Wallick and others, 2010), such data and analyses can also serve as a basis for efficient monitoring of the long-term changes in channel and floodplain conditions. This approach would be most feasible for the Broadbent Reach on the South Fork Coquille River as well as for the tidal reaches.

5. Review pre- and post-gravel-mining surveys. The review conducted for this study indicates that these surveys can provide quantitative information on bed-material deposition. In-depth and comprehensive review of all mining surveys on the Coquille River may provide better estimates of coarse gravel recruitment that can assist in constraining sediment budgets (see, for example, Wallick and others, 2011).

6. Assess bed-material composition throughout the study area. Additional measurements of particle size would be required for calculating bed-material transport and also may support assessments of temporal changes in bed-material composition in conjunction with other study components.

Detailed Channel Morphology Assessment

In this study, we delineated bar surfaces from aerial and orthophotographs spanning 1939–2009

and found that bar area declined within all fluvial reaches (tables 11 and 12). These datasets and measurements could serve as the starting point for more detailed and comprehensive temporal analyses of morphological trends in the Coquille River study area. On the basis of the findings reported here, more detailed analyses could document changes in bar area due to erosion, deposition, and vegetation establishment along previously unvegetated bar surfaces. These analyses will require accounting for uncertainties associated with the mapping protocols and differences in discharge between the aerial photographs. An approach that would meet these objectives would include the following elements:

1. Detailed mapping of land cover for multiple time periods. This effort would involve delineating the active floodplain and geomorphic features on the basis of vegetation density. Examining temporal changes in unvegetated and vegetated surfaces would allow a more quantitative assessment of channel migration, erosion, deposition, and vegetation establishment during different time periods and enable a more complete description of processes and trends of bar changes. An assessment of overall bar status and trends would benefit from supplemental bar delineations from historical aerial photographs, such as those taken in 1942, the 1950s, 1972, 1976, 1986, 1989, 1990, 1995, and 2000 (table 4).

2. Detailed mapping of channel features before and after major floods to assess the response of the channel to floods of different magnitudes and, ultimately, sediment flux and channel evolution in the Coquille River study area. Possible floods for focusing this effort include those of 1945, 1955, 1964, 1971, 1981, 1996, and 2005 (fig. 4B).

3. Assessment of the potential relationship between channel migration, large wood, vegetation establishment, and peak flows. In the Umpqua and Chetco River basins, historical declines in bar area are associated with long-term decreases in flood magnitude (Wal-

lick and others, 2010; 2011). For the Coquille River, however, decreases in bar area do not appear to be correlated with a reduction in peak flows (fig. 4B). Other possible factors include changes in the type and volume of in-channel wood as well as changes in riparian vegetation conditions. Further characterization of hydrology patterns in the Coquille River basin and its linkages with climate factors related to flood peaks, such as the Pacific Decadal Oscillation, could support inferences of likely future changes in vegetation establishment and channel planform and profile.

1. Investigation of bed-elevation changes. Modern channel surveys could be compared to historical surveys, such as the USGS profile maps, cross sections at USGS cableways, flood profiles and bathymetric surveys in the Bandon Reach (table 5), to more systematically document spatial and temporal changes in bed elevation. Such analyses would complement detailed mapping of channel and floodplain characteristics and provide insights into the factors controlling the observed changes. Properly conducted and archived, such modern surveys could also serve as a basis for the long-term monitoring of vertical channel conditions.

2. More detailed review of the data available for bridges. A review of the as-built surveys and construction plans for publicly owned bridges within the Coquille River study area may provide information sufficient to assess sediment thickness and changes in bed elevation. Investigations of construction plans and permits for county- and privately-owned bridges within the study area may also yield useful information.

Legacy and Ongoing Effects of Land Use Activities

Anthropogenic activities, such as historical forestry practices (including log drives and splash damming), dredging and wood removal for navigation, and instream gravel mining, have likely affected sediment transport and deposition dynamics in the Coquille River study area. Quantitatively assessing the past and present effects of these factors on sediment dynamics would be challenging due to likely interactions among these factors as well as their interactions with the overarching physical controls on sediment dynamics such as basin topography, channel slope, geology, and hydrology. Further investigations of fine and coarse sediment inputs associated with land use activities may provide information on the relative fluxes of different clast sizes delivered to the study area and their temporal and spatial variations. An approach for investigating the relative importance of past activities on overall sediment dynamics would be to:

1. Determine the distribution of areas of active gravel transport and deposition and analyze temporal trends in channel and floodplain morphology with respect to land-use disturbances.

2. Assess changes in bar area and channel planform near historical instream gravel mining sites with a detailed geomorphic analysis.

Priority Reaches for Future Analysis

Considering the large drainage area of the Coquille River basin and portion of the basin assessed in this study, addressing all the data gaps and analyses outlined above is probably not practical in the near future. Specific reaches, however, might warrant additional analysis because of overall geomorphic conditions and ongoing management and restoration as well as gravel mining activities.

The South Fork Coquille River, encompassing the Powers and Broadbent Reaches, would be a logical analysis area because it is an ecologically important segment of the Coquille River system. Information on coarse sediment fluxes and channel dynamics may be useful for ongoing management and restoration activities addressing riparian conditions, bank erosion, and local bed lowering within these reaches. Additionally, this section of the river, which drains the gravel-rich Klamath Mountains, has been subject to multiple anthropogenic disturbances. The Broadbent Reach, in particular, has been affected by voluminous instream gravel mining and is likely responsive to upstream basin disturbances as a result of its low gradient and unconfined floodplain.

The tidal Bandon and Myrtle Point Reaches may also be logical reaches for in-depth analysis. In these reaches, the issues would pertain more to the deposition and transport of fine sediment (and associated channel and riparian conditions and processes) rather than coarse bed material. The preliminary bar mapping produced by this study may provide a baseline for more detailed mapping of geomorphic features and estuarine habitats for the tidal reaches. Since the legacy of land-use effects in the basin has probably substantially affected fine sediment transport and deposition, the transport-limited and unconfined character of these reaches makes them responsive to perturbations in sediment loads and river flow.

Acknowledgments

The framework for this study was established with the guidance of Judy Linton of the Portland District of the U.S. Army Corps of Engineers. The study was administered by Judy Linton as well as by Bill Ryan, Pamela Konstant, and Cynthia Wickman of the Oregon Department of State Lands. Field assistance was provided by Xavier Rodriguez Lloveras, National Museum of Natural Science, Spanish National Research Council, Spain. Mike Flewelling of the Knife River Corporation provided access to the Seals Bar bed-material sampling site. Christy Leas, Oregon Department of State Lands, coordinated access to the gravel mining permit files housed at the Oregon Department of State Lands. Copies of the Benner (1991), Florsheim and Williams (1996), and Clearwater Biostudies, Inc. (2003) were graciously provided by Pamela Blake, Oregon Department of Environmental Quality. Mike McCabe, Oregon Department of State Lands, provided a copy of the Coos Bay Times (1928) article, and Dolores Knight, Coos Bay Public Library, provided an electronic copy of the McGeorge Gravel Company's site photo included in the article. The University of Oregon Map and Aerial Photography Library provided a summary of aerial photographs available for the Coquille River study area. Stephen Dow Beckham and Roxann Gess Smith permitted use of historical photographs showing splash dams and log jams in the Coquille River basin. Two colleagues provided insightful comments that improved this report.

References Cited

Amaranthus, M.P., Rice, R.M., Barr, N.R., and Ziemer, R.R., 1985, Logging and forest roads related to increased debris slides in southwestern Oregon: Journal of Forestry, v. 83, p. 229-233.

Atwood, Kay, 2008, Chaining Oregon—Surveying the public lands of the Pacific Northwest, 1851–1855: Granville, Ohio, The McDonald and Woodward Publishing Company, 267 p.

Beckham, S.D., 1986, Land of the Umpqua—A history of Douglas County, Oregon: Roseburg, Oregon, Douglas County Commissioners, 285 p.

Benner, Patricia, 1991, Historical reconstruction of the Coquille River and surrounding landscape, *in* Near coastal waters national pilot project—The Coquille River, Oregon. Action plan for Oregon coastal watersheds, estuary and ocean waters, 1988—91. Prepared by the Oregon Department of Environmental Quality for the U.S. Environmental Protection Agency, Grant X-000382-1: Portland, Oregon, [variously paginated].

Beschta, R.L., 1978, Long-term patterns of sediment production following road construction and logging in the Oregon Coast Range: Water Resources Research, v. 14, p. 1011–1016.

Buffington, J.M. and Montgomery, D.R., 1999, Effects of sediment supply on surface textures of gravel-bed rivers: Water Resources Research, v. 35, no. 11, p. 3523–3530.

Bunte, Kristin and Abt, S.R., 2001, Sampling surface and subsurface particle-size distributions in wadeable gravel- and cobble-bed streams for analyses in sediment transport, hydraulics, and streambed monitoring: U.S. Department of Agriculture Forest Service, Rocky Mountain Research Station, General Technical Report RMRS–GTR–74, 428 p.

Burns, S.F., 1998, Landslide Hazards in Oregon, *in* Burns, S.F., ed., Environmental, Groundwater, and Engineering Geology, Applications from Oregon: Belmont, California, Star Publishing Company, p. 303–315.

Clearwater Biostudies, Inc., 2003, Geomorphic and riparian assessment of the lower South Fork Coquille River—Prepared for the Coquille Watershed Association, Coquille, Oregon: Canby, Oregon, 58 p.

Cooper, R.M., 2005, Estimation of peak discharges for rural, unregulated streams in Western Oregon: U.S. Geological Survey Scientific Investigations Report 2005–5116, 134 p., accessed February 28, 2012, at *http://pubs.usgs.gov/sir/2005/5116/.*

Coos Bay Times, 1928, McGeorge Gravel Co.: Marshfield, Oregon, Coos Bay Times Golden Jubilee Annual.

Coos Historical and Maritime Museum, 2011a, A selective chronology of South Coast history—Origins to 1899: accessed February 28, 2012, at *http://www.cooshistory.org/coos-historical-maritime-museum-research-aids-1899.htm.*

Coos Historical and Maritime Museum, 2011b, A selective chronology of South Coast history—1900–present: accessed February 28, 2012, at *http://www.cooshistory.org/coos-historical-maritime-museum-research-aids-1900.htm.*

Coquille Indian Tribe, 2007, Coquille River subbasin plan: Prepared for NOAA Fisheries Service, 261 p., accessed February 28, 2012, at *http://www.coquilletribe.org/documents/Coquil leRiversub-basinplan.pdf.*

Dietrich, W.E., Kirchner, J.W., Ikeda, H., and Iseya, F., 1989, Sediment suppy and the development of the coarse surface layer in gravel-bedded rivers: Nature, v. 340, no. 6230, p. 215–217.

Dodge, Orvil, 1898, Pioneer history of Coos and Curry Counties—Heroic deeds and thrilling adventures of the early settlers: Salem, Oregon, Pioneer and Historical Association of Coos County, Capital Printing Co., 468 p.

Douthit, Nathan, 1981, The Coos Bay region, 1890–1944—Life on a coastal frontier: Coos Bay, Oregon, River West Books, 163 p.

English, J.T. and Coe, D.E., 2011, Channel migration hazard maps, Coos County, Oregon: Portland, Oregon Department of Geology and Mineral Industries Open-File Report 0–11–09, 27 plates, available on DVD at *http://www.oregongeology.org/pubs/ofr/p-O-11-09.htm* as of February 28, 2012.

Farnell, J.E., 1979, Coos and Coquille River navigability studies: Salem, Oregon, Division of State Lands, 121 p.

Florsheim, Joan, and Williams, Philip, 1996, Lower South Fork Coquille River bank stablization—Prepared by Philip Williams & Associates, Ltd., for The Coquille Watershed Association and Coos County Soil and Water Conservation District: San Francisco, California, 21 p.

Furniss, M.J., Roelofs, T.D., and Yee, C.S., 1991, Road construction and maintenance, *in* Meehan, W.R., ed., Influences of Forest and Rangeland Management: Bethesda, Maryland, American Fisheries Society p. 297–324.

Gurnell, A.M., 1997, Channel change on the River Dee meanders, 1946–1992, from the analysis of air photographs: Regulated Rivers: Research and Management, v. 13, p. 13–26.

Harden, D.R., Colman, S.M., and Nolan, K.M., 1995, Mass movement in the Redwood Creek basin, northwestern California, Chapter G *in* Nolan, K.M., Kelsey, H.M., and Marron, D.C., eds, Geomorphic processes and aquatic habitat in the Redwood Creek basin, northwestern California: U.S. Geological Survey Professional Paper 1454, 415 p., accessed February 28, 2012, at *http://pubs.usgs.gov/pp/1454/report.pdf.*

Hughes, M.L., McDowell, P.F., and Marcus, W.A., 2006, Accuracy assessment of georectified aerial photographs—Implications for measuring lateral channel movement in GIS: Geomorphology, v. 74, p. 1–16.

Jones, K.L., O'Connor, J.E., Keith, M.K., Mangano, J.F., and Wallick, J.R., 2012, Preliminary assessment of channel stability and bed-material transport along the Rogue River, southwestern Oregon: U.S. Geological Survey Open-File Report 2011–1280, 98 p., accessed February 28, 2012, at *http://pubs.usgs.gov/of/2011/1280/*

Jones, K.L., O'Connor, J.E., Wallick, J.R., Anderson, S., Keith, M.K., and Mangano, J.F., 2010, Bed-material, channel stability, and regional gravel production dynamics in Oregon coastal rivers, *in* American Geophysical Union, Fall Meeting 2010, abstract #EP31A–0726: San Francisco, California.

Jones, K.L., Wallick, J.R., O'Connor, J.E., Keith, M.K., Mangano, J.F., and Risley, J.C., 2011, Preliminary assessment of channel stability and bed-material transport along Hunter Creek, southwestern Oregon: U.S. Geological Survey Open-File Report 2011–1160, 41 p., accessed February 28, 2012, at *http://pubs.usgs.gov/of/2011/1160/.*

Klingeman, P.C., 1973, Indications of streambed degradation in the Willamette Valley: Corvallis, Oregon State University, Department of Civil Engineering, Water Resources Research Institute Report WRRI–21, 99 p.

Komar, P.D., 1997, The Pacific Northwest coast-Living with the shores of Oregon and Washington: Durham, North Carolina, Duke University Press, 195 p.

Kondolf, G. M., 1994, Geomorphic and environmental effects of instream gravel mining: Landscape and Urban Planning, v. 28, no. 2–3, p. 225–243.

Kondolf, G.M., Lisle, T.E., and Wolman, G.M., 2003, Bed sediment measurement, *in* Kondolf, G.M., and Piegay, H., eds., Tools in fluvial geomorphology: Chichester, England, John Wiley and Sons, p. 347–395.

Lane, J.W., 1987, Relations between geology and mass movement features in a part of the East Fork Coquille River Watershed, Southern Oregon Coast Range, Oregon: Corvallis, Oregon State University, Master of Science thesis, 119 p.

Lisle, T.E., 1995, Particle size variation between bed load and bed material in natural gravel bed channels: Water Resources Research, v. 31, no. 4, p. 1107–1118.

Ma, Lina, Madin, I.P., Olson, K.V., Watzig, R.J., Wells, R.E., Niem, A.R., and Priest, G.R. (comps), 2009, Oregon geologic data compilation [OGDC], release 5 (statewide): Portland, Oregon Department of Geology and Mineral Industries, available on DVD as of February 28, 2012, at *http://www.naturenw.org/cgi-bin/quikstore.pl?store=maps&product=001547.*

Mangano, J.F., O'Connor, J.E., Jones, K.L., and Wallick, J.R., 2011, Experimental attrition rates of bed-material sediment from geologic provinces of Western Oregon and their application to regional sediment models, in American Geophysical Union, Fall Meeting 2011, abstract #EP51A–0826, San Francisco, California.

MFG, Inc., Graham Mathews and Associates, and Alice Berg and Associates, 2006, Assessment of the lower Smith River—Report prepared for the County of Del Norte: Crescent City, California, 41 p.

Miller, R.R., 2010, Is the past present? Historical splash-dam mapping and stream disturbance detection in the Oregon Coastal Province: Corvallis, Oregon State University, Master of Science, 110 p.

Mount, Nicholas and Louis, John, 2005, Estimation and propagation of error in the measurement of river channel movement from aerial imagery: Earth Surface Processes and Landforms, v. 30, no. 5, p. 635–643.

O'Connor, J.E., Wallick, J.R., Sobieszczyk, Steve, Cannon, Charles, and Anderson, S.W., 2009, Preliminary assessment of vertical stability and gravel transport along the Umpqua River, Oregon: U.S. Geological Survey Open-File Report 2009–1010, 40 p., accessed February 28, 2012, at *http://pubs.usgs.gov/of/2009/1010/*.

Oregon Department of Environmental Quality, 2000, Upper South Fork Coquille water quality management plan, Coos Bay, Oregon, 68 p., accessed February 28, 2012, at *http://www.oregondeq.com/wq/TMDLs/docs/so uthcoastbasin/usfcoquille/wqmp.pdf*.

Oregon Department of Geology and Mineral Resources, 1999, Gravel mining in the Coquille River Basin, Oregon: accessed February 28, 2012, at *http://www.coastalatlas.net/metadata/GravelMi ningintheCoquilleRiverBasin.htm*.

Oregon Department of State Lands, 2007, Heads of tide: Oregon Geospatial Enterprise Office, accessed February 28, 2012, at *http://www.oregon.gov/DAS/EISPD/GEO/alph alist.shtml*.

Oregon Partnership for Disaster Resilience, 2010, Coos County multi-jurisdictional natural hazards mitigation plan: Prepared for Coos County, Eugene, Oregon, 282 p., accessed February 28, 2012, at *http://www.co.coos.or.us/ccem/Coos_County_N HMP_Final_06-21-10.pdf*.

Peck, Hilaire and Park, Chris, 2006, Hydrology report, *in* Grigsby, K., Coastal healthy forest

treatments, Environmental assessment, Analysis file, Chetco, Gold Beach and Powers Ranger Districts, Rogue River–Siskiyou National Forest, 75 p.

Phelps, J.D., 2011, The geomorphic legacy of splash dams in the Southern Oregon Coast Range: Eugene, Oregon, University of Oregon, Master of Science thesis, 38 p.

Reid, L.M. and Dunne, T., 1984, Sediment production from forest road surfaces: Water Resources Research, v. 20, p. 1753–1761.

Roering, J.J., Kirchner, J.W., and Dietrich, W.E., 2005, Characterizing structural and lithologic controls on deep-seated landsliding— Implications for topographic relief and landscape evolution in the Oregon Coast Range, USA: Geological Society of America Bulletin, v. 117, p. 654–668.

Swanson, F.J. and Dyrness, C.T., 1975, Impact of clear-cutting and road construction on soil erosion by landslides in the western Cascade Range, Oregon: Geology, v. 3, p. 339–396.

U.S. Army Corps of Engineers, 1879, Annual report of the Chief of Enginners to the Secretary of War for the Year 1879—Part II: Government Printing Office, Washington DC, 939 p., accessed February 28, 2012, at *http://books.google.com/books?id=TPYWAQA AIAAJ&pg=PA945#v=onepage&q&f=false*.

U.S. Army Corps of Engineers, 1891, Annual report of the Chief of Enginners, United States Army, to the Secretary of War for the Year 1891: Part V: Government Printing Office, Washington DC, 728 p., accessed February 28, 2012, at *http://books.google.com/books?id=BRktAAAAI AAJ&printsec=frontcover&source=gbs_ge_su mmary_r&cad=0#v=onepage&q&f=false*.

U.S. Army Corps of Engineers, 1898, Annual report of the Chief of Enginners, United States Army, to the Secretary of War for the Year 1898—Part I: Government Printing Office, Washington DC, 1074 p., accessed February 28, 2012, at *http://books.google.com/books?id=4E0tAAAAI AAJ&pg=PP5#v=onepage&q&f=false.*

U.S. Army Corps of Engineers, Portland District, 2010, Ocean dredged material disposal site management/monitoring program, summary report for the Coquille River: 7 p., accessed February 28, 2012, at *http://www.nwp.usace.army.mil/docs/d_sedime nt/odmds/Coquille_AMR.pdf.*

U.S. Forest Service, 2008, Pacific Northwest Region, Data resource management/fire a: accessed February 28, 2012, at *http://www.fs.fed.us/r6/data-library/gis/rogue-river/index.shtml.*

U.S. Geological Survey, 2010, 14325000 South Fork Coquille River at Powers, OR, *in* Water-Data Report 2010: accessed February 28, 2012, at *http://wdr.water.usgs.gov/wy2010/pdfs/143250 00.2010.pdf.*

Wallick, J.R., Anderson, S.W., Cannon, Charles, and O'Connor, J.E., 2010, Channel change and bed-material transport in the lower Chetco River, Oregon: U.S. Geological Survey Scientific Investigations Report 2010–5065, 68 p., accessed February 28, 2012, at *http://pubs.usgs.gov/sir/2010/5065/.*

Wallick, J.R. and O'Connor, J.E., 2011, Estimation of bed-material transport in the lower Chetco River, Oregon, water years 2009–2010: U.S. Geological Survey Open-File Report 2011–1123, 12 p., accessed February 28, 2012, at *http://pubs.usgs.gov/of/2011/1123/.*

Wallick, J.R., O'Connor, J.E., Anderson, Scott, Keith, Mackenzie, Cannon, Charles, and Risley, J.C., 2011, Channel change and bed-material transport in the Umpqua River basin, Oregon: U.S. Geological Survey Scientific Investigations Report 2011–5041, 112 p., accessed February 28, 2012, at *http://pubs.usgs.gov/sir/2011/5041/.*

Walter, Cara and Tullos, D.D., 2009, Downstream channel changes after a small dam removal—Using aerial photos and measurement error for context; Calapooia River, Oregon: River Research and Applications, v. 26, no. 10, p. 1220–1245.

Wilcock, P.R., Pitlick, John, and Cui, Y.T., 2009, Sediment transport primer—Estimating bed-material transport in gravel-bed rivers: U.S. Deparment of Agriculture Forest Service, Rocky Mountain Research Station, General Technical Report RMRS–GTR–226, Fort Collins, Colorado, 78 p.

Willingham, W.F., 1983, Army Engineers and the development of Oregon—A history of the Portland District, U.S. Army Corps of Engineers: U.S. Army Corps of Engineers,, Portland, Oregon, UN 24, 258 p., accessed February 28, 2012, at *http://140.194.76.129/publications/misc/un24/t oc.htm.*

Zybach, Bob, 2003, The great fires: Indian burning and catastophic forest fire patterns of the Oregon Coast Range, 1491–1951: Corvallis, Oregon State University, PhD dissertation, 451 p.